HOW TO T

AS A

Everything You Need to Know and Do
Before You Go
2021-2022

Brian and Linda Garavalia

Skye Media, LLC
Lady Lake, FL

Disclaimer

Although the publisher and the author have made every effort to ensure that the information in this book was correct at press time and while this publication is designed to provide accurate information in regard to the subject matter covered, the publisher and the author assume no responsibility for errors, inaccuracies, omissions, or any other inconsistencies herein and hereby disclaim any liability to any party for any loss, damage, or disruption caused by errors or omissions, whether such errors or omissions result from negligence, accident, or any other cause.

Published by Skye Media, LLC, Lady Lake, FL
First edition; First printing

Cover photo credit: Jonathan Korner on Unsplash
Interior photo credit: Brian Garavalia

ISBN Print: 978-1-7344845-1-9
ISBN ebook: 978-1-7344845-2-6

TABLE OF CONTENTS

TABLE OF CONTENTS

INTRODUCTION

Plan your European travels with confidence

Have you thought about immersing yourself in a European culture, living like the locals in a small European village or historic city center, adopting a new way of being, if only for a time? While this may be in your retirement dreams, and those of many Americans, have you thought about how you'd actually plan such an adventure? You may say, "Sure, I can do that!" And, then comes the actual planning. Barriers may emerge, such as, knowing about visa and passport requirements...restrictions on how long you can stay...learning how to find lodging for an extended period of time. Do US cell phones work in Europe? Will US health insurance or Medicare provide coverage in Europe? Is it best to rent a car or take public transportation? What currencies are used? How do you even begin to budget for a long trip in Europe, especially within a retirement budget?

We're here to help you make that European dream a reality with this step-by-step, comprehensive guide to spending weeks or months of your retirement in Europe. Millions of American retirees travel to Europe each year. Some travel to immerse themselves in the culture and history of charming towns and cities that date back to the ancient Roman Empire and beyond, while others seek to soak in the sun and relax in quaint cliff side villages along spectacular Mediterranean coastlines. Other retirees plan to hike through stunning alpine hillsides and flowering meadows, or to rejuvenate in gorgeous lakeside spa hotels in the shadow of the Alps. Whatever your idea of the perfect European holiday, it will surely only come true if you plan it. This guide takes the anxiety out of the planning. We're able to cover all that you need to know, because we've done it ourselves.

Over the past twenty years, we have traveled extensively through Europe, sometimes for shorter two-week trips and more frequently for months-long extended travels. This book is a compilation of things that we've learned along the way. We've done the research so that you don't have to.

We're both experienced researchers having spent our careers as professors and researchers at universities in the US.

Knowing how to identify the sites you want to see, the places you want to stay, and the experiences you don't want to miss is all part of the planning process. We'll take the guesswork out of the planning process so that you can make the most of your travels as well as your budget.

Traveling to Europe involves regulations and customs specific to each country that you visit. We provide a wealth of information to answer the questions you have and address situations that you might not have considered. This book provides loads of tips that will allow you to travel with confidence as well as peace of mind. More importantly, the information we provide is current. We'll provide updates to this book each year and to our blog site (createjoyinretirement.com) on a regular basis.

The importance of planning cannot be emphasized enough. A good plan will help you enjoy your trip long before you leave home. Anticipation is half the fun. Sometimes we plan our travels years in advance, even while we're continuing to enjoy our current trips. Those distant travels are the ones in the "dreaming" phase. They're important because they help minimize the inevitable sadness we feel when a trip is coming to an end. We know that another trip is always just around the corner.

Here's just a taste of what we cover in this comprehensive guide.

As a US citizen, you need a passport that will be valid for at least 6 months from your intended exit from Europe. Some countries only require 3 months validity beyond your planned exit date, but it's best to be safe and have at least 6 months. Carry your passport with you at all times, as police may request to see it at any time. Passports and other travel documents are discussed in Chapter 14.

When you book your travel, you need to include a return ticket home. Border control is very serious about this issue. They'll ask how you intend to return home when you reach the border of your European destination or at the ticket desk of your outgoing transportation. It sounds like a silly oint to make, but countries are leery of illegal immigrants. If you want to tay longer than the allowable tourist stay, you'll need to obtain a long-stay isa or citizenship. Visas and citizenship are discussed in Chapter 15.

e conscientious about how long you stay in a country or region. If you xceed the allowable tourist stay, you may be deported, fined, jailed, and/ r banned from the country or region for a period of years. Tourist stays re discussed in Chapter 1.

uropean countries use different currencies. Many European countries are n the Eurozone; they use the Euro as currency. The United Kingdom uses ritish Sterling (aka, pounds). A list of country currencies and tips for ob-aining cash are provided in Chapter 8.

ublic transportation is easy to use in Europe. Rail or city passes are gener-lly a great idea. Although cars are convenient for traveling at your leisure, t can be difficult and expensive to park in many of the historic towns and ity centers. Chapters 6 and 7 discuss transportation options within Eu-ope.

urope has endless options for lovely places to stay. An online travel ser-ice can help you quickly identify places that align with your preferences. However, plan to spend some time reading the reviews and considering options before actually booking your accommodations. It's also a good dea to look for bookings that allow free cancellation in case your plans hange. 'Finding the best places to stay' is discussed in Chapter 5.

You may be wondering how much does a fabulous trip to Europe cost and now can it fit into a retirement budget. See Chapter 9 for an itinerary with eal travel costs and ideas for how to scale up or down.

We hope this book will help you embark on your European travels with con-idence. You'll learn about the various types of travel documents and when you need them. Organizational tips and strategies are provided to enhance enjoyment of your travels without breaking the bank. If you want to stay for more than a long holiday, you'll particularly like our an in-depth section on strategies to remain in Europe for an extended period of time (longer han the typical 90 out of 180 days) through visas or strategic traveling

among countries. We also provide the processes for obtaining long-sta
visas, residency permits, health insurance and care, and other necessities
Although our focus is Europe, we think you'll find that the information ma
be applied to any extended trip you might undertake. Follow along, step
by-step, and start creating that European adventure. Bon voyage!

Note: Traveling to Europe during COVID-19 and post-Covid restric tions

European travel is still possible during the pandemic. Doing so in a re
sponsible, cautious manner is important. Our guide provides strategies fo
healthy, responsible travel. In general, we wear masks when we are nea
other people-- inside shops or museums, walking on busy sidewalks, rid
ing public transportation, etc. We evaluate the risk of places and choose
travel options according to how closely people are gathered, compliance
with mask wearing, and the length of time that we might be in an enclosec
space with other people.

In general, we avoid riding busses, visiting most museums, and attending
any kind of performance or crowded event. Plenty of other options fo
entertainment are available. European cities frequently have numerous
parks and are surrounded by nature with opportunities for long walks anc
hikes. Zoos are a great outdoor option for fun. Appreciate the beauty of
Europe by wandering through the historic section of town to take in the
different styles of architecture and magnificent old churches. Other activities might be similar to what you would do at home and are still fun when
traveling. For example, spending extra time lounging in the morning over
coffee and the news, relaxing over an extended lunch, reading engaging
novels, and watching binge-worthy programming on streaming services
(e.g. Netflix) are all additional fun ways to fill the day. If you view travel
as a way to enjoy life, then it's no longer important to pack each day with
sightseeing, museums, and shows. Think instead about how you would
enjoy the time at home and translate that to a fun new environment that
provides a different landscape and architecture with lots of opportunities
to observe the daily life of another culture.

CHAPTER 1:
WHAT IS EUROPE?

Chapter 1: What is Europe?

- European Union
- Eurozone
- Schengen Area
- Non-Schengen Countries
- New entry requirements for US travelers beginning in 2022
- Stay restrictions for all European countries

Stonehenge, Salisbury Plain, Wiltshire, England

After years of traveling in Europe, we've learned some lessons along the way that will hopefully help you with your European travels. Before diving into the planning details, it's useful to have an idea of the scope of Europe as a geographical area, some of the geopolitical organizations within Europe, and newly emerging requirements for US travelers.

In the seven-continent model of the world, Europe is the 2nd smallest continent comprised of approximately 50 sovereign states and approximately 750 million people. Interestingly, not everyone agrees on which countries are truly European countries. For our purposes, we take a very broad view of Europe as being the continent and its surrounding islands. It is bordered by the Arctic Ocean to the north, Atlantic ocean to the east, Mediterranean Sea to the south, and Asia to the west.

The countries can be divided into 7 geographic regions:

- Scandinavia
- The British Isles
- Western Europe
- Southern Europe
- Central Europe
- Southeast Europe
- Eastern Europe

Amsterdam, The Netherlands

For the purpose of this book, when we refer to Europe, we mean all of the above regions. A list of all of the countries is compiled for you in Table 1. Aside from knowing the European countries, US travelers should be aware of a few different sub-regions and geopolitical organizations.

European Union (EU)

Originally conceived to create a peaceful region with shared prosperity, the EU now includes 27 member states. In the late 1940s, following the second World War, 6 countries-- Belgium, France, Germany, Italy, Luxembourg and the Netherlands – formed an alliance to pursue joint prosperity through formal trade alliances. In the 1960s, members of the union began to trade across borders without charging each other custom duties. In the early 1970s, EU membership grew to 9 countries with the addition of Denmark, Ireland, and the United Kingdom.

The EU gained in popularity and political power as the last right-wing dictatorships fell in Spain and Portugal. True to the initial intent, the EU strived to support poorer areas with transfers of huge sums of money to create jobs and infrastructure. The union also created a system of representative governance for member nations and adopted laws to curb pollution by holding offending nations accountable.

Spain, Portugal, and Greece joined the EU in the 1980s. Significantly, in 1989, Germany became reunified when the Berlin wall fell. This event marked a shift in political ideology from communism to capitalism in eastern European countries with ripple effects across nearby countries over the next decade.

Temple Bar, Dublin, Ireland

In the early 1990s, the long pursued vision of a "Single Market" was realized. Member nations enjoyed free movement of goods, services, people, and money across the union. In the early 2000s, the Euro became widely adopted as currency in most EU countries.

Over time, the EU has continued to work cooperatively to overcome economic challenges and climate change. The members also work together to enable the free movement of people which allows citizens from one country to work and live in another country without the visa and work permit requirements for outsiders, such as US citizens.

At this time, 27 countries are members of the European Union. An up-to-date listing of EU countries can be found at https://europa.eu/european-union/about-eu/countries_en. A number of countries are currently seeking to join the EU. Note that the United Kingdom withdrew from the EU on January 31, 2021.

Eurozone

All of the European countries that have adopted the Euro as the official national currency make up the Eurozone. The Euro, as currency, was officially introduced in 1999 and began circulating in the early 2000s. At this writing, there are 19 Eurozone countries: Austria, Belgium, Cyprus, Estonia, Finland, France, Germany, Greece, Ireland, Italy, Latvia, Lithuania, Luxembourg, Malta, Netherlands, Portugal, Slovakia, Slovenia, and Spain.

)ther countries have their own national currencies.

chengen Area

'his border-free zone is currently comprised of 26 European countries hat have agreed to allow free movement among the Schengen member ountries. It was originally conceived in June of 1985 when 5 countries – rance, Germany, Belgium, Luxemburg, and the Netherlands – signed the chengen Agreement. It's called the Schengen Agreement because it was igned in the small village of Schengen in southern Luxemburg. Border-ree means that citizens of these 26 countries can live, work, and travel cross borders without visas or any other requirements.

or the US tourist, it's important to know about the region, because you an travel across the borders freely once you have cleared passport con-rol in a Schengen country. US citizens may travel among these countries vithout any special visas or paperwork as tourist for 90 out of 180 days.

\s a US traveler, the days of your tourism visit accrue across countries when you're n the Schengen area. For example, if you visit France for 20 days and then move on o Italy for another 15 days, you will have iccrued 35 days of your 90-day limit in he Schengen area.

Many EU countries are members of the Schengen area. Five exceptions are: Re-public of Ireland, Cyprus, Croatia, Bul-garia, and Romania. These five countries are European Union members but are not part of the Schengen area; however, Bul-garia and Romania are in the process of

Overlooking Bolzano, Italy

oining. Four countries are part of the Schengen area, but are not mem-bers of the European Union: Iceland, Norway, Switzerland, and Lichten-stein. For more information, see https://ec.europa.eu.

Non-Schengen countries

Restrictions on length-of-stay for tourists vary for Non-Schengen countries. Stay restrictions are presented in Table 1. Something to keep in mind, the British Isles and a number of other European countries are not members of the Schengen; however, they will participate in the European Travel Information and Authorisation System (ETIAS) upon implementation in the latter part of 2022.

New entry requirements for US travelers beginning in 2022

European countries will begin utilizing a new system in 2022 to deter terrorism and make Europe more secure – the European Travel Information and Authorisation System (ETIAS). US Citizens and other non-EU nationals will be required to apply to the ETIAS towards the end of 2022.The ETIAS travel authorization is a visa waiver that is valid for a 3-year period. With

Lucca, Italy

the travel authorization, US and other non-European citizens are free to travel as tourists for 90 out of 180 days. This stay restriction is the same as the current one; the difference is that travelers will now be required to complete an ETIAS application. After the 3-year period, reapplication will be required. Note that citizens of Schengen area countries and other European states will not be required to complete the ETIAS to travel as tourists in Europe.

Remember, it's the traveler's responsibility to know the entry requirements and stay restrictions for each European country. Just like in the US, compliance with the law is expected and begins with knowing the law. See Table 1 for stay limits for all European countries, both Schengen and non-Schengen.

Table 1: European Countries and Stay Restrictions for US Tourists (as of March 2021)

Schengen area countries Tourism visa is 90 out of last 180 days	Non-Schengen countries Tourism visa varies for each country	
Austria (EU)	Albania	Up to one year
Belgium (EU)		
Czechia (EU)		
Denmark (EU)	Andorra	Periods up to 3 months
Estonia (EU)		
Finland (EU)		
France (EU)	Armenia	180 days per year
Germany (EU)		
Greece (EU)		
Hungary (EU)	Azerbaijan	Up to 30 days
Iceland		
Italy (EU)	Belarus	No more than 90 days total in a calendar year
Latvia (EU)		
Lithuania (EU)		
Luxembourg (EU)	Bosnia & Herzegovina	Up to 90 days within a period of 6 months
Malta (EU)		
Netherlands (EU)		
Norway	Bulgaria (EU) (seeking to join Schengen area)	Up to 90 days within 6 months
Poland (EU)		
Portugal (EU)		
Slovakia (EU)	Croatia (EU) (seeking to join Schengen area)	Up to 90 days during a 6 month period
Slovenia (EU)		
Spain (EU)	Cyprus (EU) (seeking to join Schengen area)	Up to 90 days
Sweden (EU)		
Switzerland		
	Georgia	Up to 365 days
Vatican City treated as part of the Schengen Area for tourist visas		
	Ireland (EU)	Up to 90 days over a 6-month period
	Kosovo	Up to 90 days within 6 months
	North Macedonia	Up to 90 days within a 6 month period

Schengen area countries Tourism visa is 90 out of last 180 days	Non-Schengen countries Tourism visa varies for each country	
Austria (EU) Belgium (EU) Czechia (EU) Denmark (EU) Estonia (EU) Finland (EU) France (EU) Germany (EU) Greece (EU) Hungary (EU) Iceland Italy (EU) Latvia (EU) Lithuania (EU) Luxembourg (EU) Malta (EU) Netherlands (EU) Norway Poland (EU) Portugal (EU) Slovakia (EU) Slovenia (EU) Spain (EU) Sweden (EU) Switzerland Vatican City treated as part of the Schengen Area for tourist visas	Moldova	Up to 90 days within a 6 month period
	Monaco	Up to 90 days within a 6 month period
	Montenegro	Up to 90 days
	Romania (EU) (seeking to join Schengen area)	Up to 90 days within a 180 day period
	Russia	Up to 180 days in a row
	San Marino	Up to 90 of the last 180 days
	Serbia	Up to 90 days within a 180 day period
	Turkey	Up to 90 days
	Ukraine	Up to 90 days
	The United Kingdom (EU)	Up to 6 months in a year per stay

Summary

- If you are a US citizen traveling to Europe as a tourist, you don't need a visa unless you are planning to exceed the stay restriction in a particular country or area

- 26 European countries form the Schengen area which allows free movement across borders once you have cleared passport control in a Schengen country

- Schengen area countries have a combined stay restriction of 90 out of the last 180 days for tourists

- Non-Schengen countries vary with regard to how long you may stay as a tourist

- The Euro is used in many countries, but check the country website to identify the currency prior to travel

- Towards the end of 2022, non-EU citizens will be required to complete the ETIAS prior to travel to Europe. Successful ETIAS applicants receive a 3-year tourist visa waiver.

Monterosso al Mare, Cinque Terre National Park, Italy

CHAPTER 2:
WHAT DO YOU WANT TO DO AND WHERE DO YOU WANT TO GO?: THE DREAMING PHASE

Chapter 2: What do you want to do and where do you want to go?: The dreaming phase

- Embrace the retirement travel mindset
- Identify your travel preferences
- Describe how you like to spend your time
- Identify the best region of Europe to do your favorite things
- Decide how much time you will spend on the trip and when you will travel
- Complete the checklist for the ideal travel experience
- Review our general guidelines for travel

"Life is a journey, not a destination."
Ralph Waldo Emerson

Embrace the retirement travel mindset

Travel can be a defining aspect of your new life in retirement. It's about personal growth. It requires you to step out of your comfort zone, to do things that are different from the daily routine. An unfamiliar environment stimulates curiosity and brings a sense of independence. When traveling, you leave behind the familiar. It can be one of the most rewarding things you ever do. New experiences make you

Lake Plitvice Lakes National Park, Croatia

a more interesting person with more to share with others. You may feel excitement or even fear, but never boredom.

If you're new to retirement, this European trip that you're planning may be your first during life-after-work. Retirement travel planning is different than when you have work obligations. Most obviously, the travel will not be about work. It's also not about a vacation to escape work for a couple of weeks.It's about fun and exploration, and it can be whatever you want. The travel limitations that you lived with for years no longer apply. You don't have to select dates that mesh well with the work calendar. You don't have to limit the number of days for your trip. There will be no re-entry pain when you return to the workplace. No one will ask you to join a conference call when you'd rather be hiking or sitting by the pool. Travel will be totally different now that you are free of work obligations.

In retirement, you can go anywhere at any time. Choose to travel in high season or choose to enjoy the shoulder or off seasons when destinations are less crowded and less expensive. Take a slow boat to your destination. You can travel for as long as you'd like. Cross as many time zones as you'd

Venice, Italy

like without worrying about joining meetings back home or being too jet lagged to work. Don't worry about whether the Wi-Fi is stable enough for video conference calls or has enough bandwidth to receive large email attachments.

Recognize that you're entering a whole new phase of life where you can recreate who you are as an individual. When people ask you what you do, you say, "I'm retired." You'd be surprised at how seldom people follow up with, "Well, what did you do before retirement?" We've found that new people we meet in our travels want to know about

what we're doing now. Where are we traveling? What sights are we seeing? What types of hobbies have we picked up? Are we learning the language? The conversation has changed. It takes some time, but one day you'll realize that you no longer identify with your job title.

Now that you have no constraints, think about why you're traveling – to learn about new cultures, enjoy different cuisines, see historic sites, hike alpine trails, lounge on Mediterranean beaches, take in spectacular countryside views, maybe even learn a new language? Travel should be fun, so, during your planning, think about things that you enjoy. Sometimes the most enjoyable moments happen spontaneously, but we've found that travel is a lot more fun when we plan to have fun.

To be honest, international travels began for us well before our retirement years, tied in with work or simply for fun and pleasure. The real difference though is the length of our travels post-retirement. We're now able to enjoy months long journeys, and we frequently do!

When we first started planning our European travels, we spent hours sitting in our local book store sipping coffee and looking at guide books and magazines. We watched travel videos and tuned in to international house hunter shows, vicariously exploring housing options in Europe. We made lists of places we wanted to visit, sites we wanted to see, things that were important to us.

Bourton-on-the-Water, Cotswolds, England

Researching and talking about our future European travels became a fun hobby that we both enjoyed tremendously. More importantly, it was an affordable source of entertainment during our 'saving' days, and we could mentally escape cold winter days or stressful work as we talked and planned.

Moving from the dreaming stage to actual trip planning felt a little over-whelming at first. Luckily, we had our lists of sites we wanted to see and things that we agreed were important. Those lists helped guide our initial choices. We kept in mind that we planned to visit many places and choosing one place for a particular trip didn't mean that we would never visit another. Perhaps that's a good place for you to start as well.

Identify your travel preferences

Talk with your travel partner about travel preferences and goals. You don't have to agree on everything. We use the rule that if something is really important to one of us, then we try to accommodate it. But, just because you're traveling together, it doesn't mean that you have to do everything together. Sometimes you may want to spend an afternoon or day doing your own thing, and that's okay.

Start narrowing down your travel options by identifying what's important to you.
- What do you want to see?
- How do you want to spend your time each day?
- How much responsibility do you want to take for making arrange-ments and getting from place to place?
- How much money are you willing to spend?

The point of planning is to build in as much enjoyment as possible in advance and to avoid as much unpleasantness as you can.

If you haven't already decided on your location or the type of trip you want to take, it can be hard to know exactly where to start when planning a long trip. Here are some important factors to consider:

Temperatures at location: Cold, Warm, Hot

Europe experiences seasons at the same time as the US. Just like in the States, the further north you go, the cooler the temperatures. Look at a map to find comparable US or Canadian destinations that will help you gauge how hot or cold it will be. Check weather.com for average temperatures across the year.

You might be surprised that some places in Europe are rarely warmer than the 50s or 60s, even in the middle of summer. Ireland, Scotland, and northern England can be quite chilly during the summer. Likewise, Greece, Turkey, and southern Italy can be very hot during the summer. On occasion, Europe reports a heat wave in the summer, but it's rare. Because it never really gets hot in some regions, many places in the more northern countries or the mountains don't even have air conditioning!

Tourist season at location: Off, Shoulder, High

During work life, vacations are often during high season, meaning lots of tourists are flocking to your travel destination. If you don't mind crowds and higher prices, then it won't bother you to travel during high season.

A keen advantage of retirement is that you can travel whenever you want. Why not travel when the crowds are less and the prices are better? The shoulder season usually means that you will still have decent weather, but the crowds will be less.

If you're not worried about foul weather, then the off season is the best way to go. Sometimes attractions are closed, but most museums are open. The seaside and mountains are still there. There are less cars and busses on the road. You can get much better prices at hotels, short-stay apartment lets, and day tours. Traveling during off season is an excellent way to stretch your travel budget.

Length of trip

Go with a tour trip itinerary (e.g. cruise, bus tour, biking trip)

Tour operators and cruises offer an array of destinations and durations. You can also add days to the front and back end of the trip. Having someone else plan your itinerary is an advantage if you're new to European travel. We took a 21-day Mediterranean cruise to explore different counries before feeling comfortable enough to create our own itineraries.

Two weeks or less

Choose 2-3 places to stay that are near public transportation and then take day trips. Moving around every couple of nights is an option, but we've tried it, and it's exhausting. The fewer times that you have to tote around and then unpack your bags, the better.

Two weeks to one month

Staying a week in each locale could allow you to thoroughly explore each area, identify some favorite restaurants and bakeries, and to feel comfortable walking around the town without getting lost.

More than a month

Finding a favorite village with a lovely apartment near public transportation, restaurants, and shops is one type of heaven. If you have a chance to spend considerable time in a village, you can get to know the locals at the market and the restaurants. You'll experience setting up a daily routine and saying hello to the same people on your morning walk each day. The restaurant owners may introduce themselves and provide special treats, such as free dessert or a glass of wine, when you become a repeat patron. Consider enjoying a nice long stay in a single destination with lots of opportunities to take day trips and explore the region. Oftentimes, apartments are discounted when you stay a month.

Travel destination

Europe has everything you could want. Try to narrow your destination options by selecting the type of environment you'd like to enjoy.
- Beach, lake, or river
- Mountains, alps, or dolomites
- Cities and historic centers
- Rural villages and countryside
- Archeological parks and digs
- Bicycling routes
- ...whatever you imagine when you think of the ideal European destination

Flights to nearby major airports

The prices for airfare can vary greatly for different airports. Direct flights are often more expensive than flights with a layover or two. When you're deciding on your arrival and/or departure airport, think about whether convenience, price, or time is of the most value to you.

Many places in Europe are just a train ride away from major airports. For example, Lucca, Italy is a 23-minute train ride from Pisa airport. Pisa is a small, regional airport. You'll need to layover in a larger hub prior to flying to Pisa. However, you could also fly direct into Milan and make a 5-hour train trip to travel to Lucca. Rome could also be a direct flight and is about a 6-hour train ride from Lucca. You will usually have many airport options when you travel from the States to small European villages.

Availability of transatlantic cruise nearby

If you're willing to arrive or depart from a port that hosts transatlantic cruises, then this is an excellent option. Cruises travel from the US to Europe in April or May. They return for the Caribbean season in October or November. Typically, these cruises are not crowded. The cost is much lower than a regular cruise. All the amenities of a cruise are available, except for stops in ports each day.

A transatlantic cruise is about two weeks in duration. Think about what is included in the cost of your cruise: one-way transportation as well as food and lodging for 14 days. A room with a balcony on a decent ship will run around $8000 for a couple. That's an average of $571 per day...not bad for accommodations, food, entertainment, and transportation.

Ease of travel around your home base for sightseeing

Using public transportation

Consider how easily you'll be able to access train and bus lines for daily travel when you're deciding on a village as a home base. If you want to use a rail pass, then you'll want to choose towns that are on the rail line. If you really want to stay in one that doesn't have a train station, then look for taxis, Ubers, or bus stations. You'll be able to arrange a taxi, Uber, or bus to and from the nearest train station to your small village. You'll find that the European bus system is fairly comprehensive, so you should be able to get wherever you want to go by bus.

Renting a car or hiring a private driver

Consider the ease of parking and navigation when renting a car. Be aware that in some of the smaller European villages you need a permit to drive in the historic center. Parking almost always costs. Different countries have different strategies for collecting your payment, but it's almost always a self-service box. Note the number of your parking space, and then find the payment box. Usually, you will be able to use a credit card (Visa or Master-card) or debit card.

Don't expect to have free parking or parking next to your accommodation. You might be able to drop off your bags nearby, but then you will need to drive to the nearest parking area. Keep in mind that road signs will be in the local language. Use a GPS that will give you directions in English and, hopefully, alert you to the meaning of any road signs (e.g. bridge out ahead, road closed).

If you want to travel by car, a private car and driver might be a good option. Search for private car services online and then read the reviews. If there are no or few reviews, you probably don't want to take a chance on that service.

Type of trip you prefer

You have many options. Decide on one and then start planning. Here are some examples of your options:

- All-inclusive travel tours (e.g. bus tours, biking tours,
- cruises)
- Cruise-- ocean or river
- Pre-planned itinerary set by travel agency, online bloggers, or guide-book
- Nomadic roaming self-planned itinerary with brief stops in multiple places
- Long-stay rental in a quaint home-base city or village
- Caravan/RV rental
- Glamping
- Study abroad for older adults (e.g. Road Scholar)

Extra-friendly options for the budget
- Camping
- Agritourism opportunities
- Volunteer your time and services in European locales
- Swap houses with a European
- House and/or pet sit
- Stay in Pensions or Hostels
- Travel from monastery to monastery
- Take a Pilgrim's walk

Budget preferences

Work with your travel partner to agree on a budget range for each of the major expenses involved in travel

- Airfare or cruise fare
- Nightly accommodations
- Meals, groceries, and snacks
- Day trips and guided excursions
- Concerts, museums, attractions, national parks
- Train and/or bus fare, Ubers, guided tours

Describe how you like to spend your time

Is your perfect day filled with museum visits or hikes through nature? Do you prefer to sunbathe on the beach or browse through the upscale shops on the Champs Elysees? Are historic centers with old cobbled streets and quaint architecture appealing?

The first step to deciding where you want to visit in Europe is to imagine your perfect vacation day. Your preferences in Europe might be similar to your preferences for US vacations. Below are some ideas to help you think

Conwy Castle, northern Wales

about the things you like to do. Check all of the things that are appealing to you and your travel partner(s).

- Wander through the historic sections of medieval cities
- Visit museums, archeological sites, historic homes, palaces and chateaus
- Have lunch and a glass at wine at a cute bistro in a quaint village or square
- Play golf or tennis
- Visit a zoo or go on a safari
- See a matinee
- Enjoy an evening at the theatre followed by a fancy "apres theatre" dinner
- Spend a day at an amusement park
- Lounge by the swimming pool or the seaside
- Create some art, throw some pottery, or learn how to make mosaics
- Relax at a yoga retreat
- Run a 5K in a new city
- Go mountain biking or take a biking tour through the countryside
- Hike from village to village in the Alps or along the Cinque Terre
- Take walking tours with narration of the historic buildings and monuments
- Go rappelling or abseiling down cliff sides
- Explore caves and grottos
- Book a boat to enjoy fishing, snorkeling, deep sea diving
- Take language or cooking classes to immerse in the culture
- Hop on the ferry to spend a day on a nearby island
- Partake in all sorts of water sports – parasailing, kayaking, paddleboarding, swimming, jet skiing
- Go horseback riding
- Ski the Alps
- Take a canal cruise
- Book a barge and bike tour
- Enjoy a river cruise
- Go wine tasting/or become your own personal sommelier
- Learn how to be an olive oil taster

Identify the best region of Europe for doing your favorite things

One strategy to focus your destination is to assign a theme for your trip. Work with your travel partner to decide what type of trip appeals the most to all involved. Work together to find common ground on the desired level of activity, the amount of buzz near your home base, and the immersion in culture or nature. Here are some ideas for themes:

- Alpine hikes and mountain views
- Lakeside retreat
- Historic city centers and their museums, architecture, shops, and restaurants
- Biking trip through the countryside
- Cruise down European rivers
- Bike and barge tour
- Wine or olive oil tasting
- Language and/or other cultural learning programs
- Religious pilgrimage

Take time to write down the countries you'd like to visit and the historical sites and cultural experiences that are your top priorities. Look through guide books at a book store. Search the Internet. Ask your friends about their favorite places in Europe.

Verona, Italy

Here's an example to help you get started:

Country	Historical sites and cultural experiences
Germany	• Rhine river cruise to see the castles • Christmas market in Munich • Guttenberg printing press in Mainz • Imperial Roman baths of Trier • Remains of the Berlin wall and Checkpoint Charlie • Bruhl Palaces in the northern Rhine region • Schwerin Castle on the island • Neuschwanstein Castle (the Disney castle) in Bavaria
France	• Paris o Eiffel Tower o Louvre o Champs Elysees o boat ride on the Seine o Notre Dame Cathedral o Montmartre o Palace of Versailles • Loire valley chateaus • Cote d'Azur o Cannes o Saint Tropez o Antibes o Nice o Monaco (really a separate state from France) • Mont Saint-Michel and abbey church • Provence • Chamonix – Mount Blanc • Villages
Italy	• Cinque Terre • Rome o The Colosseum o The Pantheon o The Capitoline o Villa Borghese Gardens o Trevi Fountain o Il Gelato di San Crispino

Country	Historical sites and cultural experiences
Italy	<ul><li>Cinque Terre</li><li>Rome</li><ul><li>The Colosseum</li><li>The Pantheon</li><li>The Capitoline</li><li>Villa Borghese Gardens</li><li>Trevi Fountain</li><li>Il Gelato di San Crispino</li></ul><li>The Vatican (a separate state from Italy surrounded by Rome)</li><ul><li>St Peter's Basilica</li><li>hear an address by the Pope</li></ul><li>Florence</li><ul><li>Santa Maria del Fiore Duomo</li><li>Accademia Gallery</li><li>Boboli Gardens and Pitti Palace</li><li>Michelangelo's David</li><li>Palazzo Vecchio</li><li>Uffizi Gallery</li><li>Ponte Vecchio</li><li>Mercato Centrale</li><li>Take an olive oil tasting class</li></ul><li>Venice</li><li>Naples and the ruins of Pompeii</li><li>Sorrento</li><li>Capri and Anacapri</li><li>Sicily and Mount Etna</li><li>Take a boat ride around Lake Como</li><li>Visit a winery in Chianti</li></ul>
The Netherlands	<ul><li>Amsterdam</li><ul><li>The Anne Frank House</li><li>Museums in the Museumplein</li><ul><li>Van Gogh museum</li><li>Rijksmuseum</li><li>The Royal Concertgebouw</li></ul><li>Visit the Brouwenj't IJ microbrewery under the windmill</li><li>Take a canal cruise</li><li>Visit the Royal Palace Amsterdam</li></ul><li>The Hoge Veluwe National Park</li><li>Visit the tulip fields</li><li>Keukenhof Gardens</li><li>Rotterdam</li></ul>

Country	Historical sites and cultural experiences
The Netherlands	• Delft • Maastricht • The old windmills of Kinderdijk • Haarlem • The Hague Alkmaar Cheese market • The Efteling • The New Dutch Water Line • Waddenzee • Giethoorn

Here are some more ideas for interesting sites and cities to see in Europe. Look them up on the Internet if you need more information. Check all the places and sites that appeal to you.

• SeteCidades&Lagoa do Fogo, Sao-Miguel- Azores- Portugal
• Santa's reindeer in Rovaniemi, Finland
• Meteora, Greece
• Canals of Amsterdam
• Krka National Park, Croatia
• The Bosphorus, Istanbul, Turkey
• Zakynthos Island, Greece
• Lake Plitvice, Croatia
• Tea on a boat tour on the Thames, London, England
• Benagil Caves, Carvoeira, Algarve
• Giant ferris wheel in Vienna, Austria
• Porto, Portugal
• Dordogne Valley, France
• Eiffel Tower, Paris, France
• Leaning Tower of Pisa, Pisa, Italy
• Bled, Slovenia
• Bom Jesus do Monte, Braga, Portugal
• Northern lights, Reykjavik, Iceland
• David in the Galleria dell'Accademia, Florence, Italy
• Burano & Murano Islands, Italy
• Capri and Anacapri, Italy
• Christmas markets in Germany
• Salzburg, Austria
• Waltzing in Vienna, Austria

- St. Petersburg, Russia
- Lofoten Islands, Norway
- Cornwall, England
- Calpe, Spain
- Cappadocia, Turkey
- Ghent, Belgium
- Rhine river, Germany
- Tubingen, Germany
- Canary Islands, Spain
- Soca Valley, Slovenia
- Kotor, Montenegro
- Kefalonia Island, Greece
- Sibiu, Romania
- Dalmatian Coast (Split, Dubrovnik, Cavtat), Croatia
- Rome, Italy
- The Vatican
- Nerja Beach, Andalusia, Spain
- St Nicholas Island, Montenegro
- Santorini, Greece
- Crete, Greece
- The Cote d'Azur, France
- Mamaia Beach, Romania
- The Amalfi Coast, Italy
- Menorca and Mallorca Islands, Spain
- Bolata Beach, Bulgaria
- Venice, Italy
- Sintra, Portugal
- Aix-les-Bains Riviera of the Alps, France
- Biarritz, France
- Bruges, Belgium
- Budapest, Hungary
- Bergen, Norway

Historic city center, Belgrade, Se

Add any sites that you've found in your research or that have been on your radar as must-see destinations. Hopefully, the sites you and your travel partner identify and the activities that you prefer have some overlap and are compatible.

Before moving on to the next step, start to narrow down your lists. Decide

Tenby, southern Wales

which sites and activities you want to do on your next trip. Save the other preferences for later trips.

You may also want to consider your budget when you're deciding on your travel region. Some cities in Europe are definitely less expensive than others. Here's a listing from least to most expensive to give you an idea about where your money might go further.

Least to most expensive cities

1. Prague, Czech Republic
2. Belgrade, Serbia
3. Istanbul, Turkey
4. Lisbon, Portugal
5. Berlin, Germany
6. Barcelona, Spain
7. Dalmatian Coast (Split and Dubrovnik), Croatia
8. Rome, Italy
9. Munich, Germany
10. Paris, France
11. London, England
12. Dublin, Ireland
13. Amsterdam, Netherlands
14. Geneva or Zurich, Switzerland

Decide how much time you will spend on the trip and when you will travel

Review your calendar for the upcoming year. Decide which family and friends events need to be considered. Evaluate how you want to spend holidays, birthdays, and other special days. Decide if you want to travel in high, shoulder, or off season.

An important axiom to keep in mind is that 'less is more'...don't try to see everything in one trip. If you enjoy traveling to Europe, you can find ways to enjoy it again on another trip. Here are some general guidelines for how to plan your time.

7 days – 2 cities or one city with day trips
10 days – 3 cities or two cities with day trips
14 days – 4 cities or a road/train trip through one or two countries

Don't forget to factor in travel time – plan about 4 hours between cities. If you are taking an extended trip through Europe, consider establishing a home base and making day trips to see the surrounding region. A benefit of staying a month or more is that you can likely rent an apartment for much less than paying nightly hotel rates. Sometimes, we even travel overnight to other places while maintaining our home base. That way, we can just carry a small bag and leave the rest of our belongings in our home base.

Creating the ideal travel experience

Consider your adaptability to variations in your daily routine and living situation. Start with our checklist of options and then decide if each is an essential, would-be-nice, or not necessary alternative for your travel. Add anything that's important to you in creating the ideal travel experience.

Creating the Ideal Travel Experience Checklist	Essential	Would-be-nice	Not necessary
Airfare options			
1. Flat-bed seats for transatlantic flights			
2. Europe business class for flights within Europe			
3. Regular seats with extra legroom			
4. Meals included			
5. Direct or one-stop			
6. Short layovers			
7. Access to an airline lounge			
8. Extra support for people with mobility limitatins			
9. Accommodations for pets			
10. Minimal baggage fees			
11. Minimal add-on fees for seat assignments, boarding priority, carry-on luggage			

Creating the Ideal Travel Experience Checklist	Essential	Would-be-nice	Not necessary
Transportation to accommodations			
1. Affordable taxi or Uber fares from airport			
2. Public transportation available			
3. Hotel shuttle available			
4. Budget shuttle available to more distant locales			
Convenience of accommodation location			
1. Near public transportation			
2. Parking available			
3. Within walking distance of grocery and dining			
4. Near laundry facilities			
5. Near water, hikes and walks, historic sites and/or other attractions			
Comfort of accommodation			
1. Comfort of bed (e.g. firmness, bedding quality)			
2. Size of bed (e.g. king, double)			
3. Noisiness of area, hotel, or room			
4. Free Wi-Fi			
5. Enough room for adequate personal space/size of lodging or travel arrangements			
6. Air conditioning and heating			
7. Kitchen/refrigerator/microwave			
8. Coffee maker/water kettle			
9. Washer and dryer			
10. Accessible bathroom/roll-in shower			
11. Bathtub			
12. Smoking or non-smoking			
13. Fireplace			
14. Outdoor space			
15. Beautiful views			
Food Preferences and Tolerances			
1. Exoticness of flavors and dishes			
2. Types of meats and vegetables			
3. Timing and frequency of meals			

Creating the Ideal Travel Experience Checklist	Essential	Would-be-nice	Not necessary

Fitness level and health limitations
1. Moving from transport to lodging with baggage
2. Walking on cobblestone streets, dirt paths, steep inclines and declines
3. Climbing uneven steps or lots of steps
4. Access to regular medications
5. Importance of specific dietary needs
6. Medication regimen
7. Hearing and sight challenges
8. Mobility
9. Breathing issues (e.g. asthma)
10. Allergies

Personal Preferences for Interaction with Others
1. Tolerance for crowds
2. Tolerance for extended time with others
3. Need for conversation
4. Need for company/companionship
5. Need for alone time

General categories of services & accommodations
1. All-inclusive resorts and cruises
2. Camping, hostels and other budget friendly options
3. Budget hotels, pensions, or hostels
4. Moderate luxury
5. Deluxe luxury

Other things that could be important
1. Free cancellation
2. Pet friendly
3. Breakfast included
4. Hot tub
5. Pool
6. Spa
7. All-inclusive plan available
8. Casino

What other adaptability options can you think of that might impact your enjoyment of travel? Add those to the list.

Mobility Limitations

Just like in the US, people with mobility limitations are traveling. In Europe, you'll see people using wheelchairs, scooters, walkers, canes, guide dogs, and sight-assist canes. It's up to you, the traveler, to decide what you're comfortable doing. We've seen very elderly people taking daily walks at a snail's pace along the cobbled streets, yet nonetheless getting in their daily walk. Ferry personnel assist wheelchair bound travelers in boarding the ferries. Busses frequently have ramps that lower to the ground to make boarding and disembarking easier. Don't hesitate to ask for assistance or for an alternate route to reach a site. On occasion, we see a notice that a site is not accessible, but it's rare. To maximize your comfort and peace of mind, explore transportation options prior to arriving in a village or city to make sure that you feel confident in getting around.

Chester Cathedral, Chester, England

Review our general guidelines for travel

Now you have a comprehensive list of things to consider when you're making travel arrangements. The key is to know what's important to you before you start booking. In addition to those specific items in our checklist, here are a few of the general guidelines that we always follow when we're planning a trip and traveling from place-to-place:

- Ensure safety first in all things – transportation, lodging, dining, and sightseeing

- Minimize hassles as much as possible

- Travel in affordable comfort within the allocated budget

- Let someone else do the driving (i.e. use public transportation)

- Enjoy local food, but don't gain weight. Eat main meal at breakfast or at lunch. Consider time restricted eating or the 5:2 fasting strategy.

- Sleep well (book accommodations with comfy beds, air conditioning, quiet space, blackout curtains)

- Travel light. Pack only what is needed. Plan to discard items along the way and buy more clothes, as needed. We have on occasion while traveling across seasons mailed back home our out of season clothing.

- Avoid accumulation of more stuff (i.e. don't buy lots of souvenirs)

- Exercise daily

- Use free WiFi to stay connected with family & friends via video calls

- Plan one to two major sites or activities per day. Don't overdo it. Less is more.

- Pay for a tour or guide when necessary to see difficult to reach places or when expert guidance would be desirable.

Church of San Pietro (1277 AD), Portovenere, Cinque Terre National Park, Italy

CHAPTER 3:
WHO'S DOING THE PLANNING AND WHERE ARE YOU GOING?

Chapter 3: Who's doing the planning and where are you going?

- Ponder planned itineraries vs free-form travel
  - Let someone else plan your trip
    - Pros and Cons of Cruises
    - What's included in the cost of the cruise?
    - Other organized trips
  - Plan Your Own Trip: Nomadic roaming or day trips from a home-base
- Choose your European travel destination for your trip
- Just do it! Plan your trip to Europe
- Example 8-week European
- Itinerary
- Extra: Tips for Planning a Well-Coordinated Group Trip

Ponder planned itineraries vs free-form travel

If you're still on the fence about what type of trip to take, the main factor to decide is whether you want to take a trip that someone else has planned

or one that you have organized. The following sections provide more insights into those travel strategies.

Let Someone Else Plan Your Trip

Cruises, bus tours, university-sponsored alumni and friends tours, "bike and barge" tours, Road Scholar and self-improvement special interest tours/cruises are just a few of the options you might consider. We strongly recommend an organized tour for your first trip if you are unfamiliar with Europe. Our first lengthy European trip was a 21-day Mediterranean cruise. The cruise originated in Rome and then toured western Mediterranean ports:

Civitavecchia (Rome)
Monte Carlo
Barcelona
Mallorca
Tunis
Palermo
Naples

Then the ship docked in Civitavecchia (Rome) for a night before embarking on the tour of the eastern Mediterranean ports:

Messina
Dubrovnik
Katakolon
Santorini
Kusadasi
Istanbul
Malta

The cruise was an amazingly easy way to visit a number of countries in a safe, efficient and cost effective manner. Following are some of the pros and cons with cruises:

Cruise Pros

- Pre-planned itinerary of popular places to see in a region.
- Your bed follows you wherever you go.
- Unpack once and don't worry about packing up and moving everything from place to place.
- The ship provides access to quality excursions/tours in English.
- You have peace of mind that you are being taking care of by the cruise line when you are on their tours.
- Currency exchange is available at the front desk if you want to get a

small amount of local currency prior to disembarking in ports.

- Alerts are shared when and where you should be extra cautious with regard to pick pocketers or other potential safety and security issues at various ports.
- Food and water are almost always safe on the ship so no need to worry about food or water-borne disease and illness.
- Exercise options are plentiful and usually include gyms, exercise classes, deck walking, swimming, and many other activities in the on-shore excursions.
- Dining options have evolved over the years. You can sit at a table by yourself or with a regular group of diners at a specified time. You can enjoy on-ship restaurants for a small extra fee, just as you would visit a restaurant anywhere. Buffets are available with a range of seating inside and out. Room service is always available.
- Security screenings are completed each time passengers disembark and embark to ensure the ongoing safety of all.

Cruise Cons

- The biggest problem for us is the fact that you arrive in port with a traveling city of people, and that can be overwhelming and bothersome to the locals. Some ports, like Venice, have even banned cruise ships because of the damage that over tourism is doing to their ecosystem and economy.
- Ships, of course, dock in large ports, which means that travelers may miss out on some of the more rustic, culturally interesting locations.
- Cruises travel on specific dates with pre-planned itineraries, and these might not suit your specific needs.
- It's possible for illness to spread rapidly through a cruise ship.
- It can be difficult to understand the pricing. Talk with the cruise/tour line, choose the options you prefer, and then ask for a final cost with a list of inclusions and exclusions.

Another wonderful aspect of booking a cruise or all-inclusive tour is that your trip is almost fully paid prior to departure. It's possible to put your wallet away and enjoy the trip without having to spend lots of money each day.

On our 21-day Mediterranean cruise, we only spent an extra $600 above the total cost of the cruise and excursions. We purchased wine cards on board ship for wine with dinner, and we enjoyed frequent lunches ashore. There are other ways that you can spend money on board with very expensive spa treatments and products, on-board photography, art sales, casino gambling, exercise classes, and other extras, but they aren't necessary to fully enjoy your cruise.

What's included in the cost of the cruise?

When you book a cruise, be sure to find out what is included in the price. Here are some of the extras that may or may not be included:

- Airfare
- Transfer from airport to bus/ship
- Meals/snacks/beverages (alcoholic and/or non-alcoholic)
- Excursions/tours/guides
- Entertainment (movies, plays, shows)
- Equipment rentals (e.g. diving or snorkeling gear, jet skis, bikes, wet suits, ATVs)
- Lessons (e.g. cooking, history, art, agritourism)
- Exercise (e.g. hikes, workouts, yoga, strength training, gym access)
- Gratuities for tour or cruise staff
- Internet access
- Bottled waters

Similar pros and cons would apply to any organized tour, whether it's a biking holiday, bus tour, or traveling classroom. The distinguishing factor is that someone else has spent the time organizing the trip and making sure that the plans are safe, enjoyable, and carried off as sold. As with any travel booking, read plenty of reviews before making your final decision.

Other Organized Trips

Whether it's active travel that floats your boat or bus tours with other retirees, there's something for everyone when it comes to booking travel in Europe. Among the active travel options are walking, hiking, and biking tours. For most of these tours, you'll have a guide or two, and they are responsible for making your life on the European road easy and enjoyable. Usually, your luggage is transported from one accommodation to the next, while you participate in your chosen activity of the day. You will want to select a company that will allow you some flexibility in your activities and provide support in case you aren't up to covering the distance for the day. Some of the benefits of seeing Europe on foot or bike are that you get a different experience of the culture. There's time to stop and take photos without a boatload of people doing the same. You can stop in the villages along the way and spend some time hunting for truly unique souvenirs without a crowd. On top of all that, you are getting in some healthy exercise.

Giant's Causeway, Northern Ireland

Maybe you would like to spend some time exploring and developing skills in a particular hobby. Maybe you've always wanted to know how to cook authentic cuisine from your favorite European country. Wine tasting anyone? Have you always wanted to play Europe's best golf courses? All of these are options when it comes to travels that are organized for you by people who are experts in whatever you want to do or learn. Plus, you will meet other travelers who share your same passions. Truly, the possibilities are endless.

Your organized tour transport may be a bus, a motorcycle, a bike, a horse, or your own two feet. The important part is that someone else has taken on the burden of making all of the arrangements for eating, sleeping, and getting you from point A to point B.

Plan Your Own Trip: Nomadic roaming or day trips from a home-base

If you only have a couple of weeks, you may be tempted to roam from city to city, changing hotels every couple of nights. We've traveled that way in the past, and found it to be exhausting. Aside from the tiresomeness of packing and unpacking every couple of days, we became very fatigued with carrying our luggage from place to place. No matter how efficiently we pack, the bags are still heavy and cumbersome. It's much easier to identify a home base, learn about that area, and enjoy lots of day trips to nearby sites. Here are some guidelines for creating your own travel itinerary:

Be organized

- Create a document to keep track of your reservations with essential information and costs. It evolves into your itinerary for the trip and can also be a document of spending to keep track of the budget.

- Make notes as you do your research. Keep a notebook or electronic notes of what you find in your searches for best airfares or cruise fares, etc. Everytime you find something to consider, make note of it. For example, if you find reviews about a quaint village in France that looks like a lovely place to visit, make note of it. To be even more organized, divide your notes into sections...transportation ideas, potential lodging options, places to visits, excursions and activities, restaurants, etc.

Identify your travel dates

- How long will you travel? Will you be traveling long enough to need someone to watch your home while you're gone? How long are you comfortable being away from home?

- What are the limitations for your travel dates? Consider special events that you don't want to miss at home.

- Is weather important to you? Keep in mind that prices are higher and crowds are largest when the weather is the best.
- Family travel is higher when school is not in session. Tourist crowds are larger when more families are traveling. Cruises are also more crowded.

Identify your destination, transportation, and lodging

- Research your options. You can travel from the US to Europe by plane or boat. Usually, transatlantic cruises sail to Europe in April and sail from Europe to the US in October and November.
- Book your travel from home to your initial European destination
- Research and identify your lodging for the night you arrive. Decide how long you will stay in that location.

Choose your European travel destination for your trip

So far, we've identified a number of factors that you might consider in planning your trip. Now it's time to identify exactly where you want to go in Europe. An obvious first issue is budget, but it's really not as important as you might think. You can go almost anywhere in Europe with a budget of just about any size. In the 1970s, Frommer's published books to help travelers enjoy Europe on $5 and $10 a day. You probably can't get by with those types of prices (unless you're willing to be a travel chaperone or a house/pet sitter), but you can certainly travel on $100 or less per day. More important issues are the amount of time you have for your travels, mobility limitations and transportation, and the types of activities you enjoy and sites you want to see.

One way to identify a worthy travel destination is to find out where other people are going each year. The top 10 most visited countries in Europe in 2020 were
   France – 86.9 million
   Spain – 81.8 million
   Italy – 58.3 million
   United Kingdom – 37.7 million
   Turkey – 37.6 million

Germany – 37.5 million
Austria – 29.5 million
Greece – 27.2 million
Russia – 24.4 million
Portugal – 22.2 million

If you want to see the more famous and popular sites in Europe, then you can't go wrong with following the crowds.

Now sit down with a cup of coffee or glass of wine and think about where you want to go and what you want to see on your next trip. Brainstorm with your travel partner or on your own. Use the Internet to help you identify the must-see places in each country. Create a table in a Word document on your computer or make notes in a good old fashioned spiral-bound notebook that you can carry with you when you visit the coffee shop or relax on your back deck. Set aside some time for your travel dreams each day or week and grow your list of places to see and things to do.

Just do it! Start making reservations and booking travel

The very first thing that you will likely book is your air or cruise travel. Buying these tickets sets the parameters for your dates of travel…your transport to and from Europe 'bookend' your travel. You need to know those dates before making other arrangements for lodging and subsequent travel within Europe. Here are some reminders from other chapters:

Traveling by air: If you plan to fly to and from Europe, then you can save money just by buying during an optimal window in advance of your trip. When do you need to buy tickets to get the best price? Optimal flight purchase times can vary widely. We advise booking airfare at least three to six months in advance. Travel and Leisure Magazine says the best fares are purchased around 160 days in advance of travel.

Keep in mind that fares vary greatly for different cabins (i.e. economy, premium economy, business, first class). If you want to spend the least amount of money on airfare, then book the economy class, but be sure to add in the surcharges when planning your budget (checked baggage fees, seat assignments, priority boarding, food and drink). The cheapest fare may actually be premium economy when you consider the extra charges with the main-cabin fare.

You could also consider the budget airlines. We have flown budget airlines within Europe, and have had good experiences. However, those are short flights. Think carefully about how much discomfort might be involved with less leg room, tighter seats, and more people in a small space if you're flying for 7 to 11 hours from the US to Europe.

Think also about purchasing a refundable fare if there is any chance that your travel plans could change. Refundable fares cost more, but it's the safest way to protect your investment in airfare.

If you can swing it financially, we highly recommend the flat bed seats in the business class section. The fares vary tremendously so look at lots of options before selecting your flight. It's worth the investment of time and patience. Consider calling the airline to see if they can find the best deal for you. Also, the two round-trip ticket strategy that we described in the 'how to get to Europe' chapter can save you lots of money. If you're flying business class, you'll save on baggage fees and airport lounge access preflight and during layovers. The food, which is free, is generally very good in the lounges and on the plane. Movies and TV are plentiful and free. The beds and blankets are quite comfortable. It's easier to arrive at your destination refreshed and happy if you've been able to sleep comfortably for part of the journey.

Traveling by sea: A transatlantic cruise is a good option if you're going to Europe in the spring or returning in the late fall. A veranda cabin may run between $6000-$8000 for two people which is probably less than flights for two people, meals for 14 days, and lodging for 14 days. If you have an unlimited amount of time and no constraints on your dates of travel, a transatlantic repositioning cruise there and/or back could be a good option. We traveled back from Europe one year on the Princess Cruise Line from Rome to Ft Lauderdale, departing from Rome (Civitavecchia) at the very end of October. We thought it was a very economical and comfortable way to get home.

As you start booking your travel, you'll want to keep track of everything in an organized manner. We keep track of everything in our itinerary in a Word document that we save to Google drive. Since our itinerary is saved to the cloud (Google drive), we can access it anywhere we have an internet connection.

You may want to print a hard copy of your itinerary to carry with you. I keep a printed copy in my purse and in my carry-on luggage. I always save a copy to the cloud in a Google folder that both Brian and I can access. Within the itinerary, I write notes to myself about how to do things (like ride the subway), directions to places, and any additional information that I think we may need.

Sometimes changes to the itinerary occur while we're traveling. We're able to update our plan as we go and keep track of booking reference numbers, payments, accommodation addresses, travel documents, and any notes for things to remember. Don't count on remembering things that are several days away...write them down.

In this chapter, we've asked you to consider a lot of different factors that affect your travel decisions. Are you ready to start the actual planning process?

Start by creating a word document or excel spreadsheet to create the skeleton of your itinerary. This initial draft will identify the dates and destinations and possibly how you plan to get from one place to another. Continue to add to the document as you make reservations and learn information that is important (e.g. how to use your rail pass, how to get from the arrivals hall in the airport to the train station).

The travel itinerary begins as a skeleton of dates and places to stay. Here's an example from one of our previous trips...

Europe 2019 August 14 – October 9

August 15 to October 9	Buy a Eurail Pass with 3 months validity
Aug 14	Arrange for ride to airport or take shuttle bus Buy airfare Orlando to Gatwick roundtrip
Aug 15-16	Arrive Gatwick Stay in London. Book hotel.
Aug 16-17	Take Eurostar to Paris Stay in Paris. Book hotel. Book air from Paris to Pisa Take Pisa airport shuttle to train. Take train to Lucca. Walk to apartment. Get directions for best route.
Aug 17 – Sept 14	Book apartment in Lucca
Sept 14- 16	Take train from Lucca to Cinque Terre Book hotel in Cinque Terre
September 16- 17	Take train to Sorrento Book hotel in Sorrento
September 17- 20	Take ferry to Capri Take bus to Anacapri Book hotel in Anacapri
September 20-21	Take bus to Capri port Take Ferry to Naples Take the train from Naples to Paestum Book hotel in Paestum
September 21-24	Take train from Paestum to Lecce Book hotel in Lecce
September 24-27	Train to Bolzano Book hotel in Bolzano

September 27-29	Train to Verona Book hotel in Verona Train from Verona to Milan to Cuggiono
Sept 29 – Oct 1	Book hotel in Cuggiono
October 1-4	Train to Turin Book hotel in Turin
October 4-7	Train from Turino Porto Susa to Paris Gare Lyon Book hotel in Paris
October 7-9 Monday day	Take Eurostar from Paris Gare du Nord to London Take the train to Windsor/Eton Riverside Book hotel in Windsor/Eton
October 9	Train from Windsor to Gatwick Fly home from Gatwick Arrange for airport pick up or take the shuttle bus

Extra: Tips for Planning a Well-Coordinated Group Trip

No one likes to experience hassles or ill-conceived activities when travel-ing. If you're planning a group trip, making sure the details are well coor-dinated is essential. If you're the person in charge of planning, you likely don't want to face the blame if things don't go well. Following these tips for planning can make your job easier and the trip more enjoyable for all involved. (These tips assume that all travelers are of adult age and can be expected to pay for at least some of the travel expenses)

Salisbury Plain, England

Tip 1: Decide what kind of trip the group prefers

A great way to narrow down the options is to have a brainstorming session followed by a process to reduce the ideas. Choose one of the travelers to lead the session and one to record the ideas that emerge. Make it fun by hosting a lunch or dinner and asking all involved to think about their ideal answers to pertinent questions. Brainstorm, with no judgment, and record the group answers to questions like the following:

- How many days?

- What type of trip—relaxing on the riviera, all-inclusive luxury resort, ocean cruise or river cruise, ground bus tour, camper van tour of na-tional parks, self-created itinerary/tour of European capitals, etc?

- How will you travel to the destination(s)? Car, plane, boat, bus, train, bicycle, motorcycle, or other transport?

- Will you choose one home base or move from place-to-place throughout the trip?
- Will everyone eat meals together? Dine out or cook at home?
- What is the general budget per person?
- How much group versus individual time will be built into the plan?
- Repeat the brainstorming session if it seems like your fellow travelers still need to explore options. After the brainstorming, create a summary of the responses and share with all involved. The brainstorming leader should then guide the decisions to travel options that appeal to all involved.

Tip 2: Identify the primary planner and his/her responsibilities

The primary planner will guide the planning process. The travel plan may ideally include input from all travelers, but it's not absolutely essential. Indeed, it may be easier if the primary planner is given leeway to create a basic framework for the trip and then solicit input for the specifics.

For example, the primary planner may suggest a group Mediterranean cruise. If all travelers are on board, then the primary planner can start researching options and developing a general plan for the trip. The primary planner might

- determine which travel items need to be agreed upon by the group (e.g. flight times, pre or post-cruise accommodation rentals, group excursions, group meals),
- research and communicate options for travel, activities, meals that involve the whole group,
- solicit and incorporate feedback for all group plans to create buy-in from fellow travelers,
- provide an itinerary to the group explicitly identifying group versus individual itinerary items,
- organize and communicate with the group during the trip to keep the plan on track.

Tip 3: Set clear expectations for financial commitments for each traveler

Once the framework for the trip has been determined, a budget should be set. The primary planner may survey fellow travelers to identify and propose a budget to the group or another traveler in the group may take on the task of researching costs and putting together a budget. Include all major expenses in the proposed budget, such as

- air, train, boat, or car fare,
- accommodations,
- transportation during the trip from place to place,
- excursions or activities,
- meals.

The process for determining the budget will vary depending on the expectations for each traveler. For example, if an individual has invited the other travelers, perhaps he/she is picking up the bulk of the travel expenses, but has the expectation that travelers will pay for meals, souvenirs, and activities. If everyone is contributing equally to, say, renting a beach house, then calculate the obligation per traveler.

Enjoyment for the group may be enhanced by following a democratic process to identify the basic parameters of the trip, these valuable tips can help you create a travel plan that takes into account the desires of each traveler and optimizes buy-in to the final plan.

CHAPTER 4:
GETTING TO EUROPE

Chapter 4: Getting to Europe

- Identify the desired conditions (e.g., convenience, cost, time, comfort) of your flight
- Airlines that fly from the US to Europe
- Cheapest time to travel to Europe
- How far in advance to book your flights to Europe
- The cheapest flight destinations in Europe
- Book a budget-saving transatlantic cruise

You have two options for traveling to Europe from the States. You can fly, or you can take a ship. Commercial travel is much, much more affordable than private jets or yachts, so we're limiting our suggestions to commercial options.

Identify the desired conditions of your flight

Possibly the biggest expense in your European travels will be airfare. Consider a number of factors when you're deciding which cabin fare to book. First, the comfort of your flight to Europe can impact the first few days of your trip. You'll be jet lagged no matter what, but you can minimize the aches and pains you might accumulate from sitting in an uncomfortable middle seat or being scrunched in an economy seat with no leg room.

Nowadays, airlines tack on all sorts of fees to economy fares...priority boarding, baggage fees, preferred seating placement, seat assignments, food and drink, etc. It may well be worth paying up front for premium economy, or even business class, when you add in all of the surcharges and the cost of discomfort. As one of my friends said about a bad flight once, "I'd pay anything to NOT be having this experience." Think carefully about what you're willing to endure for a lengthy flight across the ocean.

When searching for flights, it usually takes us several hours, sometimes days, to identify the best premium economy or business-class seats at the best price, but it's worth it to us. If you fly business class, you have entry to the airport lounges (free food and drinks!), priority boarding, free baggage allowance, and, theoretically, your bags arrive at baggage claim in the first batch.

Before you start your search, make a few decisions.
Complete the following table...

On what dates do you want to travel? How long will you be gone?	
Are your dates flexible? Can you travel on the less expensive mid-week days (Tues, Wed, Thurs)?	
How far away is your nearest US airport? Which airports would be good alternatives? List the airport codes in your order of preference.	
How will you get to your US airport?	
How much will it cost?	
If you drive, how much does parking cost?	
Which airport in Europe is closest to your destination?	
List other airports that are within an acceptable train or bus ride.	
Which cabin fare will you book (e.g. business, premium economy, economy)?	
How much are round trip flights from your home airport to one of the NYC airports, Chicago, Boston, Miami, or Atlanta airports?	
Is it less expensive for you to fly roundtrip to one of these large airports and then book a separate roundtrip ticket for the international portion of the trip?	
Which airline do you prefer?	
Can you use frequent flyer miles or credit card reward points?	

Once you've answered all of the above questions, start your search. A good place to start actually is Google Flights. A Google search will provide the best fares and flight durations for many airlines. It's easy to make changes to your search and continually refine your search options.

After you have priced flights from your home airport to your desired European airport, research a few other options.

1. Book two round-trip flights -- one domestic and one international

For example, we could travel to Paris by booking a round-trip from Orlando to JFK and then booking a second round-trip ticket from JFK to Charles de Gaulle (Paris) airport. Be careful in the time allotted for your layover though. The airline will not be as willing to assist you if a flight is late, and you miss your connection. Also, you will need to pick up your bags at baggage claim and recheck them at the ticket counter in between flights. Plan at least 3 to 4 hours for your layover or plan to stay overnight and enjoy the sites in your connecting city.

2. Book two round-trip flights – one international and one within-Europe flight

This option is a twist on option 1. Start with a direct flight toEurope from your home airport and an add-on round trip to your final

destination. For example, we can fly direct to London from Orlando. If we buy round-trip direct flights to London, we then buy another ticket -- a round-trip flight from London to Pisa for our final destination of Lucca, Italy.

Compare the cost of the two round-trip

Brussels, Belgium

flights to the cost of one round-trip booking. Choose the one that best meets your needs. Remember, you'll need to pick up your bags and go through border patrol at your European entry airport. After clearing border patrol and customs, you'll go the ticket counter and recheck your bags to your final destination.

Of course, it's easier if you just have carry-on baggage.

3. 'Open jaw' flights arrive in one city and depart from another

You can use this strategy to save time during your travel. There's no need to loop back to the starting point of your travel if you use an open-jaw flight. However, these flights are usually more expensive than roundtrip. It might be worth the extra expense if you are seeing the sights you want to see and saving time by avoiding the replication of returning to your arrival destination.

Airlines that fly from the US to Europe

Some of the full-service airlines that fly to Europe are:

Aer Lingus	Aeroflot	Air Canada	Air France
Air Italy	Air New Zealand	Air Serbia	Air Tahiti Nui
Air Transat	Alitalia	American Airlines	Austrian Airlines
Azores Airlines	British Airways	Brussels Airlines	Condor
Delta Airlines	Emirates	Eurowings	Finnair
Iberia	Icelandair	Jet Airways	KLM
LOT Polish Airlines	Lufthansa	SAS	Singapore Airlines
SWISS	TAP Air Portugal	TUI,	Turkish Airlines
United Airlines	Virgin Atlantic	WestJet	XL Airways

Unless you fly a budget airline, you'll find that the fares across the full-service airlines are usually similar. However, several airlines frequently offer deals from the US. For deals, do some research for flights on American, United, Delta, KLM, Air Canada, British Airways, and Lufthansa.

Once you have an airline and flight identified, you can either go to an online travel agency (e.g. Booking.com, Kayak, Expedia) or go to the airline website to book the flight. We have used Expedia frequently in the past with some success and some disappointment. Read up-to-date reviews of the online travel agencies before using one to book your flights or accommodations. When we book through an airline, we prefer to use Delta and its partners, but sometimes the fares are better within Europe on other airlines.

Once you're in Europe, you may find that a train or bus ride is better (faster, less costly, more convenient) than an additional flight. Check your options. We recommend that you purchase a Eurail Global pass if you think you will be taking the train across multiple countries while you're traveling in Europe. If you buy the pass before you leave home, you'll be able to use it when you land to travel from the airport to your final destination at no extra cost.

Cheapest time to travel to Europe

Airfares will be most expensive during high season. For Europe, high season is June through August and the Christmas to New Year's holiday season. Airfares will be lowest when fewer people are traveling to Europe (low season), which is November through February (except for the holidays). The other months are called 'shoulder season.' March

Kew Gardens, London, England

through May and September through October are good months to travel because the weather is usually okay, and the prices are a little better than during high season. Also, the tourist sites are less crowded.

How far in advance to book your flights to Europe

Travel and Leisure magazine recommends booking 160 days in advance to get the best fares to Europe. The least expensive fares are usually for travel on Tuesday, Wednesdays, and Saturdays, but any weekday is usually cheaper than a weekend flight. Here are some booking strategies for less expensive fares to Europe.

- Depart Wednesday, return Tuesday
- Use hubs as launchpads
- Book six months out
- Travel during the tail end of summer

You might also consider buying fares that are refundable. The cost is greater than non-refundable fares, but the pandemic has taught us that factors beyond our control can ruin our travel plans. Best to have the option to get your money back if you are unable to travel for some reason.

The Cheapest Flight Destinations in Europe

- Dublin, Ireland DUB
- Rome, Italy FCO
- Budapest, Hungary BUD
- Athens, Greece ATH
- Berlin, Germany Tegel (TXL), Schonefeld SXF, Brandenburg BER
- Paris, France. Charles de Gaulle Airport (CDG); Orly Airport (ORY)
- London, England. Airports: Heathrow LHR and Gatwick LGW
- Prague, Czech Republic. Prague Václav Havel Airport (PRG)
- Moscow, Russia SVO & DME
- Istanbul, Turkey IST and ISL
- Milan, Italy MXP & LIN
- Madrid, Spain MAD
- Warsaw, Poland WAW
- Barcelona, Spain – El Prat airport

Book a budget-saving transatlantic cruise

Transatlantic cruises are a great option if you're traveling at the time when they are sailing, and if you don't mind spending two weeks of your travel at sea. They are also called repositioning cruises, because the ship is sailing away from one area in order to provide cruises in another area. Popular European repositioning cruises sail from the Mediterranean (e.g. Rome, Barcelona) to the Caribbean (e.g. Florida) in October or November. The repositioning cruise back to the Mediterranean is usually in April or May.

You can take the cruises both ways if you are staying abroad for 5 or 6 months and can travel when the ships reposition. Otherwise, you'll need to book a flight for the other leg of the trip.

We call cruises budget savers, because they are a relatively inexpensive way to combine luxury transportation with two weeks of food, lodging, and entertainment. The actual price of the cruise varies greatly depending on the type of cabin you book, but everyone enjoys the same food, entertainment, and views, regardless of cabin cost.

It can be difficult to narrow down the options for a cruise that will fit your needs and budget. Here are some ratings from the Internet...

Best Luxury Cruise Lines	Best Cruise Lines for the Money
#1. Viking Ocean Cruises.	#1. Royal Caribbean International.
#2. Seabourn Cruise Line.	#2. Celebrity Cruises.
#3. Crystal Cruises.	#3. Norwegian Cruise Line.
#4. Regent Seven Seas Cruises.	#4. Princess Cruises.
#5. Azamara Club Cruises.	#5. Carnival Cruise Line.
#6. Oceania Cruises	#6. Holland America Line.
#7. Silversea Cruises	#7. MSC Cruises.
	#8. Costa Cruises.

Now, here are the cruise lines that offer transatlantic cruises…

- Azamara
- Cunard
- Norwegian Cruise Line
- Oceania Cruises
- Princess Cruises
- Carnival
- Celebrity
- Holland America
- MSC cruises
- Regent Seven Seas Cruises
- Royal Caribbean International
- Seabourn Cruise Line
- Viking Ocean Cruises
- Windstar Cruises. Get away from the crowd and journey to unique destinations aboard Windstar's intimate small ships.

We've taken one repositioning cruise and thoroughly enjoyed the ride. An advantage was that we adjusted to the time change as we made our way across the ocean. By the time we arrived home, we were already acclimated to our home time zone. Be sure to research options for traveling home from the port. In Florida, a "cruise bus" is a great way to get from the port to your home town. The bus dropped us off at the McDonald's near our home, and we took an Uber the rest of the way home.

CHAPTER 5:
FINDING THE BEST PLACES TO STAY

Chapter 5: Finding the best places to stay

- Create a draft itinerary with sites to see and things to do
- Identify your home-base for each area you will visit
- Identify filters for your online search
- Use an online travel agency or apartment booking service

The "best" place to stay is one that fits your needs – your budget, your personality, your preferences – and adds to the enjoyment of your travels. Where you stay can make your travel experience a joy or a hassle-filled nightmare. Moreover, lodging is one of the biggest expenses in your travels.

Spend ample time researching your options. Imagine yourself and your travel companion spending time in the area. What will you enjoy doing each day? How much do you want to spend? In this chapter, we present many of the things you'll want to consider before committing to your lodging.

Create a draft itinerary with sites to see and things to do

It can feel overwhelming making so many choices about transportation, lodging, tours, restaurants, activities...the draft itinerary allows you to create without commitment. Each time you add something to the draft, sit with it for a while to see if it feels right. Calculate the time it will involve to do the things you're considering. How much will it cost? Will your travel partner enjoy it as much as you?

Here's an example table for Florence, Italy to help you create your draft itinerary:

Date	Sights to see	How much time is required?	What's the cost?
Day 1	Florence Duomo and Baptistery	1 full day	"OPA Pass € 18 (one ticket for Baptistery of San Giovanni, Santa Reparata, Giotto's Bell Tower, Brunelleschi's Dome and the Museo dell'Opera del Duomo). The ticket allows the holder to visit all the monuments within 72 hours of visiting the first one. Each monument may be visited only once with the ticket. Reservations required for the climb on the Dome, recommended for climb up the Bell Tower and the Museum. Reservations are free and not mandatory for the last two."
Day 2	Uffizi and Accademia Gallery with Michelangelo's David		Approximately $100 per person
Day 3	Pitti Palace and Boboli Gardens		"** Special discount of 50% off the cost of the ticket if you buy before 9am and enter by 9:25am, year-round ** Combined ticket for Palazzo Pitti + Boboli Gardens + Uffizi Gallery, valid 3 days and with priority entry: from March 1-October 31 = Full € 38, reduced € 21 and from November 1- February 28/29 = Full € 18, reduced € 11"
Day 4	....continue adding sites		

Creating your itinerary may seem time-consuming, but the investment in time will help you enjoy your actual travel experience. A little planning goes a long way. You'll be able to wake up each day with a clear idea of what you're doing, where you're going, and how much it costs. Don't book any lodging until you are clear about what you want to do each day. Keep in mind that your lodging may be one of the last things you decide.

Work with your travel partner to create a list of all the places you want to go, sites you want to see, experiences you want to enjoy on this trip. Even if you think the activity or place is inaccessible, write it down if it's important to you. Worry about the 'how' later. For now, focus on the 'what.'

A draft itinerary can help you imagine yourself in different locations, how you'll be spending your time each day, traveling from place to place. In the draft, you can enter time estimates for travel between places and wandering around sites. Instead of moving from place to place, you might decide to stay in one place and thoroughly explore a region with day trips.

If you have a lot of time and are enjoying the planning process, you could create an inspiration board. Cut pictures from magazines or print them from the Internet. Look for articles that describe the destination and read reviews from other travelers.

Do you have more places on your wish list than days? Narrow down your list of places. Select what you can't miss and what you think won't be that spectacular. Consider distances between destinations, and make sure everything makes sense. Prioritize the order of the places you want to visit.

Avoid overplanning-- don't jam pack each day with tons of different activities and sites. People often think that the more things they pack into a day, the better the trip. When you're traveling, this approach can be exhausting. The point of travel is to experience other cultures, to enjoy other ways of being, to learn about the world, and to see new things. Travel is not a contest to see

The Bell Inn, Moreton-in-Marsh

who can be the most "productive" by seeing the most sites. When it comes to enjoying travel, less is definitely more.

Lastly, when you're creating your draft itinerary, build in some flexibility. Invariably, flights or trains will be delayed. The weather will fail to cooperate. Sites may be unexpectedly closed. You might wake up feeling poorly one morning. You'll be jetlagged and sluggish at times. Build in some time to allow for a change of plans if things don't go as you expected or you don't feel like tackling the day's activities. Consider including days in your draft itinerary where you simply enjoy the area around your home base. There's no need to wander far and wide every day.

Identify your home base for each area you will visit

Once you have created a draft itinerary, decide on the specific towns/cities for your lodging. Can you stay in one place and see all of your sites from one home base? Think about the time you might save by taking day trips instead of actually moving from place to place.

Location: Your optimal location is going to depend on how you're traveling. If you have a car, then you may want to stay in the countryside where the prices for lodging are lower. Find a town where you can take the train or bus into the city. It's notoriously difficult to park in European cities and villages so it's not a great idea to plan to rent a car and then drive in the cities. In many instances, you'll need a special permit to drive in tourist areas, such as historic city centers.

An easier option is using public transportation. Stay close to train and/or bus stations in the city centers if you want to stay where the action is, but still want to easily explore other places within the region. Another advantage of staying in city centers is that you can walk to restaurants and interesting sites, rather than paying for taxis or other transportation throughout your stay.

Castle Hotel, Conwy, Wales

Do your research: Use the Internet to explore the area as much as you can before you make a final decision about where to stay. If you don't know anything about the town or city, start with Wikipedia. You can find information about the demographics, the history, the climate, and other things that might impact your travel enjoyment. Search online for the town chamber of commerce or tourism office. Read online articles about the city or village. Read reviews and recommendations in TripAdvisor and in Rick Steve's chat rooms. Use Google Earth to see a satellite view of the area around your potential accommodations (e.g. Does the area look clean? Are there shops and restaurants on the street? Is it on a busy road?) If no one is writing about the area, then there is probably a reason that they are not visiting and writing. Stick with tried and true places when beginning your European travels.

Identify nearby sites and activities: Think of your hotel or apartment as a home base. From there, you can sightsee around the immediate surroundings or take busses or trains to nearby villages, cities, beaches, etc. Think about how you want to spend time each day. What kind of routine do you want to create that makes the experience similar or different from being at home?

Here are some examples of things that might be important to you:

- Opportunity to exercise daily (e.g. easy access to pleasant walking or biking trail in nature setting, gym with cardio equipment and weights, a number of flights of steps to access lodging, nearby walkable city streets or country lanes, hike-able mountain trails, swimming pool, beach with long walkable boardwalk)..

- Walkability to restaurants and attractions

- Outdoor temperatures (spring like temps or winter snow?)

- Quiet place and time to drink coffee and read the news (electronically) in the morning.

- Access to public transportation to enjoy nearby villages, cities, and attractions easily

- Ease of driving and reading road signs

- Quality restaurants that are relaxing, good value for the money, and nice ambience for lunches

- Comfortable accommodations to relax in the evening with your streaming services on a smart TV along with a comfy bed

- Vibrant nightlife options nearby

Personally, we search for apartments or hotels that are a) within walking distance of the train station (i.e. within 1 km or about ½ a mile), b) are located near or within the historic district, c) are walkable – nearby restaurants, shops, and sites, and d) are safe and quiet, as indicated by reviewer comments.

Identify filters for your online lodging search

The property doesn't have to be a 5-star hotel to be lovely and stylish in Europe. Use the ratings of reviewers to develop a picture of the accommodation and the neighborhood. If you can map the address, use the Google Earth satellite view to check out the surrounding area. Look for green space, sidewalks, traffic, nearby restaurants/groceries. Look for graffiti on the walls of nearby buildings. How pristine would you like the area to be?

Before you start looking make a list of things that are important to you. What attributes of the accommodations, neighborhood, city would you prefer? Sometimes you can use these things as filters in a search engine. Examples:

- Cost per night including fees and taxes.
  - Is a damage deposit required in addition to room cost?
  - Be sure to check the total cost in small print to make sure the price per night is accurate once fees and taxes are included. Sometimes the total cost is double the per night cost once you add in additional fees.
- Kitchen
- Laundry facilities
- Reliable, free WiFi
- Apartment, home, hotel, campsite, camper van, cruise cabin
- Accommodations that are allergen-free to the extent possible (e.g.

no carpeting, no pets allowed, regular cleaning available)
- Smoking or non-smoking
- Air conditioning
- Quiet area or sound mitigated lodging (e.g. noise blocking windows)
- Windows that open (with screens?)
- Outdoor sitting area or garden with nice views and landscaping
- Number of bedrooms and bathrooms
- Type of bed (king, double, twins)
- Tub/shower combo or walk-in shower
- Within 1 mile of the train station or equivalent transportation/Walkable access to public transportation
- Within the historic center, near a city park or lake, near walking paths, etc.

Reviews: Whatever you do, take the time to read the reviews. I have a new rule for our travel -- a property must have no fewer than 20 reviews. Be sure to read the negative reviews closely. I especially like properties that have hundreds of reviews. It's obviously much harder to fake that many reviews.

Free cancellation: Prior to the pandemic, I almost always booked the lower cost non-refundable rate. Now, I am booking free cancellation options only. Be sure to check the amount of notice you must give for free cancellation. Usually a 24 or 48 hour notice is reasonable. Some places have a 30 or 60 day notice required. Be careful about booking those properties if the travel situation could change without much notice prior to your stay.

Use an online travel agency or apartment booking service

Online travel agencies or booking services make it very easy to book your own travel. TripSavvy lists the following top sites for 2021:

- Best Overall: Booking.com
- Best Budget: Skyscanner
- Best Package Deals: Expedia
- Best for Reviews: TripAdvisor
- Best in Asia: Agoda
- Best in Europe: Lastminute.com
- Best Secret Deals: Hotwire
- Most Innovative: Kiwi.com

For apartment rental services, here are some good options:

AirBnB – Connects hosts with people who are looking to rent a room or an entire property. They provide a secure messaging platform for communication between hosts and guests as well as a secure payment system. AirBnB has instant booking and 'request to book' options.

HomeAway – Operated by Expedia. Be careful about these properties as reviews are vetted before being allowed. That means negative reviews may be excluded. Also, these properties almost always have a large service fee, cleaning fees, and/or damage deposit. HomeAway will usually let you book shorter stays – minimum of 3 nights, for example. Be careful and look at the bottom line cost for the property. It may actually be double the per night rate after you add in all the fees.

VRBO – Offers a wide selection of properties, but has the same issues described above for HomeAway (lots of fees). Watch out for the cleaning fees and damage deposits. Also, we had a terrible experience with VRBO in Zagreb, Croatia. The customer service team told us that the host had 24 hours past our check in time to make the apartment available to us. We ended up finding a hotel. VRBO finally refunded us when the host failed to make the apartment available, even after the 24 hours. We don't recommend VRBO, but we still use it when we can't find other good options in an area.

VacationRentals.com is geared more towards budget-conscious travelers, but the prices are not necessarily better than other sites. The stay requirement may be longer than VRBO or HomeAway. Watch out for additional fees that may automatically be added – trip insurance, accidental waiver fee.

Sykes Cottages is a small company in the United Kingdom that specializes in private homes. It's difficult to communicate with the staff on the phone, but the website allows you to view properties, make your booking, and submit your payment.

FlipKey was owned by TripAdvisor. It offers "rentals and private rooms for every kind of trip." Ratings appear with pictures of the properties. Again, watch out for added fees.

Booking.com is a good option because it provides listings for hotels, apartments, bed and breakfasts, hostels, etc. Use the filters to narrow down your search. You may be able to get discounts if you join their mailing list. This site frequently offers good 'deals.'

OneFineStay caters more to the luxury market. It provides concierge services, like at a hotel, a personal greeting upon arrival, fresh linens and toiletries, and 24/7 support. You can pay for additional services including airport transfers, childcare, and grocery delivery. The rates tend to be higher, but the quality is quite good.

9flats-- small short-term rental site with all owner-occupied listings. Nicer properties. Prices are in euros so be sure to do the conversion to US dollars when you're deciding if it fits your budget.

Wimdu is "Europe's biggest portal for city and holiday apartments." Wimdu features properties all over the world and has verified properties and owners. A tax/service fee is added to the total as well as a currency conversion fee if you're paying with American dollars.

Priceline is a great search engine to find last minute deals. It has a "name your price" feature that is good if you have a little time to wait for your booking. The advertising claims that you can get hotel rooms for steep discounts at the last minute.

www.hostelworld.com is a great site to explore if you're on a tight budget. They list private rooms as well as dorm beds in backpacker hostels.

Consider staying in monasteries if you like peaceful, austere surroundings. Consult Monasterystays.com for numerous options.

Lucca Apartments and Villas (luccaapartmentsandvillas.co.uk) for gorgeous properties in Lucca, Italy.

CHAPTER 6:
TRAVELING WITHIN EUROPE

Chapter 6:
Traveling within Europe

- Regional flights
- Traveling by train
- Taking the bus
- Subways and trams
- Ferries and river boats
- Hiring a car and driver or renting a car

Regional flights

If you're traveling long distances within Europe, flying is probably your best bet. For example, a train trip between Paris and Rome will take 15 to 20 hours, whereas a flight will be less than 2 hours.

Flights between Schengen Area countries of Europe are not regarded as international flights. Once you have cleared border control within the Schengen Area, there are no further Immigration controls and no customs within the EU as you move among the countries.

Being at the airport 2 hours ahead is good, just as in the US. You may experience long lines at security, and that can add to your time, but no more so than in the US. Just like in the US, it depends a lot on the airport, time of day, and the day of the week. Be sure to take all liquids out of your carry-on bags, purse, etc., including hand sanitizers. All liquids need to be of the acceptable size and placed in one clear, quart-sized plastic bag.

Be prepared to place all of your technology in bins as you clear airport security. That includes iPods, iPads/tablets, possibly cell phones, laptops, possibly voltage converters, and possibly all technology plugs. It varies by airport, so pack all of that stuff together and be prepared to remove those items from your carry-on bag. Avoid packing any technology and other valuables in your checked baggage. Just as in the US, theft from checked bags happens.

When you're searching for flights, you may prefer to fly with major carriers. Kayak identified the best airlines in Europe in 2019. The following airlines received the highest marks as the best airline...

Airline	Score
SWISS:	80.8%
Lufthansa:	79.5%
Turkish Airlines:	79.1%
SAS:	77.3%
Aegean Airlines:	76.1%
Aeroflot:	76.1%
Austrian Airlines:	76.1%
KLM:	76.0%

"Best" means flights are usually on time, seldom cancelled, and have good service. Before booking a flight, be sure to read the reviews for the airline. Sometimes you won't have a choice as to which airline you fly. For example, in Croatia and Serbia, you might be limited to their home country airlines for shorter flights, unless you're willing to make long detours to hubs for other major airlines. We've flown both Air Croatia and Air Serbia and were very happy with both experiences. Just because an airline is smaller doesn't mean it will be less efficient or poorer quality. Again, read traveler reviews.

To find the best prices for flights, consider using a metasearch engine, such as Skyscanner or Adioso.

Skyscanner is easy to use and quotes the cheapest prices found on the web. They check many, many airlines. It's an especially great tool if you don't have fixed plans. A particularly valuable feature is being able to search for flights to an entire country rather than a city. If you really don't know where you want to go, you're able to search for flights to "everywhere," which allows you to choose a destination by cost of getting there.

Adioso is also a good search tool. Of the two websites, Adioso gives you a much wider range of search options. You can search for flights between two specific dates, and you can even search for flights to "somewhere warm" or "somewhere within five hours."

A word of warning if you're booking flights on low-cost carriers. Surcharges can quickly add up and make the actual fare much more expensive than the initial low base fare. In addition, all of the budget airlines have their own rules on what is considered "carry-on" luggage. Charges for checked luggage can be very high. Also, you may be charged extra for a seat assignment, for heavy checked bags (e.g. more than 45 pounds), and boarding passes printed at the airport.

Low-cost airlines generally require online check-in prior to arriving at the airport. You'll need to either print your boarding pass before you arrive at the airport or download it onto a smartphone. In contrast, full service airlines will let you check-in at the airport kiosks or a ticket counter. You can still check in online, but you don't need to worry about finding a printer for your boarding pass or being unable to access your boarding pass if your phone battery dies while you're waiting to board.

Be sure to compare the cost of flights with train travel. If you're traveling through the UK and considering taking the Eurostar to Paris, you may find that it is less expensive to fly. However, if you have a Eurail Global pass, then you'll only need to pay the cost of the reservation, which would make the Eurostar less expensive than airfare.

Also consider the actual time involved in flying. A 1-hour flight takes up to 4 hours once you include the transportation to the airport, 2-hour check-in, the actual flight, then more time at the airport walking to baggage claim and collecting bags. Airports are typically located a distance from the city center, so consider the amount of time and money taking a bus, train or taxi from and into town.

Lastly, flying over Europe is not the same as being able to enjoy the scenery from your train, bus, or car window. You'll miss out on part of the European experience. A train ride lets you relax, read, chat, meet people and experience Europe. Consider your transportation between destinations as sight-seeing.

Traveling by train

Many travelers consider the train to be the best way to travel from city-to-city in Europe. You'll find that train travel is a part of the European way of life, and sometimes crowded with locals using it as their everyday way of getting around. Train rides are an experience, and you might just find that they become a highlight of your trip. Trains have a number of advantages over other forms of travel in Europe. As a traveler, the stress is less because...

Electronic arrivals and departures board

- Trains travel from city center to city center so no need to find transportation to and from an airport outside of the city.
- Seats generally have plenty of legroom.
- Store your luggage on designated racks, allowing you to keep your things near you at all times. Plus no worries about packing liquids in plastic bags and no limits on liquid size.
- Stand up whenever you'd like.
- Walk to the bar or restaurant car for food or drink (if available).
- Walk to the restroom at any time.
- Bring your own picnic on board, including alcohol.

A word of caution though from experience, as with any form of mass transit, delayed departures and arrivals can happen, so plan your connecting trains accordingly with time buffers or options for connections.

Europe has a vast rail network covering almost every town & city, with a range of departures every day. Trains run at up to 320 km/h, which is almost 200 mph. It's faster than flying for many journeys. Here are some typical train travel durations:

London to Paris (2h20)

Paris to Amsterdam (3h20)
Paris to Geneva (3h05)
Barcelona to Madrid (2h38)
Rome to Venice (3h45)

Even longer train rides, such as Paris-Barcelona (6h20), are better by train. Consider that you'll enjoy great scenery while traveling from city center to center. The alternative is about a 5-hour experience taking the regional train from Paris city center to one of the airports, complying with the 2-hour check-in guidance, taking the flight, navigating the airport in Barcelona, then reading signs in Spanish to find the metro into the city or paying for an expensive taxi.

For longer train rides, you might enjoy sleeper trains, which cover long distances while you sleep. Think of traveling from Paris-Venice, Zurich-Prague or Prague-Krakow. Consider that you are saving the cost of a hotel as well as saving daylight time when you can be sight-seeing instead of traveling.

To buy train tickets, you have three options: pay-as-you-go for tickets bought in advance, tickets purchased at train station or on the train on the day of travel, or a train pass. In general, it's cheaper to book your outward journey and return at the same time (Be sure to say that you want to include "return" if buying at the station). You can usually specify that you want to return "anytime" on a given day to avoid having to decide exactly which train you'll be hopping.

Book in advance

Most major cities in Europe are connected by high-speed trains. Tickets for high-speed and long/medium distance trains are usually variably priced, which means the price is determined by route popularity, distance traveled, and when the ticket is booked. The factor that impacts price the most is how far in advance you book the ticket. Earlier booking equals cheaper tickets. The difference can be substantial. A ticket between Paris and Amsterdam can vary between €35 and €120+ if booked at the last minute.

Try using a third party booking website to purchase European train tickets. These sites are more user-friendly than booking through each country's national rail service. They also have the advantage of selling tickets for multiple country rail services. Keep in mind that there is a small service charge (€2 to €3), but they don't mark up the actual ticket prices. Some good sites are Omio, Trainline, and RailEurope.com. We've used Trainline many times with good outcomes. Also, keep in mind that some countries charge extra for reservations when you have a rail pass, so don't be surprised when there is a cost for a ticket.

If you choose to use national rail service sites, the best sites are:

- Austria National Rail
- The United Kingdom National Rail also try Virgin Trains
- France National Rail (it may try to redirect you to RailEurope; choose voyages-sncf.com)
- Germany National Rail
- Ireland National Rail
- Italy National Rail
- Sweden National Rail
- Switzerland National Rail

It's advisable to book at least one month in advance to get the best ticket prices. Most national rail services start selling train tickets 60-90 days before the date of departure.

If you want to travel from London to Europe on the train, you'll be taking the Eurostar. Buy direct from their website (https://www.eurostar.com/uk-en). Tickets are on sale 180 days in advance, and you should buy tickets as soon as possible. Ticket prices can vary greatly. For example, a Eurostar ticket purchased 3-4 months in advance will cost around $70 while a ticket purchased the day of departure can cost $300. Also, if you have a Eurail Global pass, you can book a seat on the Eurostar, but you need to make a reservation and pay the reservation fee. Be sure to book your reservation well in advance. We traveled on the Eurostar in 2019 with 1st class Global Eurail passes, and the cost was about $75 per seat.

Buy at the station or on the train on day of travel

Some trains operate on a fixed-price ticket, meaning that the ticket cos
the same no matter when you purchase it. All domestic trains within Be
gium, Luxembourg, the Netherlands, and Switzerland are fixed price; r
reason to book ahead. Just show up at the station, buy your ticket, and g
on the train.

If you do buy your ticket at the station, don't expect the person at th
counter to speak English. Be prepared by writing down the destination an
train time for the ticket you'd like to purchase. Remember that Europea
trains times are in military time (e.g. 8 pm = 20:00) If you are returnin
indicate that you want to purchase the outward and the return tickets. Yo
can use Google translate to figure out how to write your request in th
local language.

Be sure to allow time for long lines at customer service windows. You ca
always make a trip to the station ahead of travel to buy your ticket at a
off-peak time. Also, you can use the ticket machines, but they frequentl
will not accept US credit cards. Sometimes you can use cash (local cur
rency).

Eurail Pass

The easiest way to travel by train in Europe is to buy a Eurail pass. Eurail i
the rail pass for overseas visitors. You can buy a Eurail pass if you reside ir
the US. These passes cover unlimited train travel either in the country o
your choice with a Eurail single-country pass or across most of Europe witr
a Eurail Global pass.

A pass is not necessarily the cheapest way to travel, but we've found it
to be the absolute easiest way to manage our train travels. In our experience with train stations, lines to buy tickets can be quite long and hectic. If
you're in a hurry, and time is short, having a rail pass in-hand allows you to
go directly to the train and board, avoiding the extra hassle factor.

Eurail is not a train operator; the pass can be used on any and all of the
regular trains run by the participating operators. See the Eurail site for
the participating operators. A day on a pass allows unlimited travel from
midnight to midnight (or beyond midnight when using a sleeper train). It
only covers the national rail operator(s). Taxis, buses, airlines, metro trains

(subways) or trams, and the RER trains in Paris are not included.

A Eurail single-country pass now exists for each participating country except Switzerland & Germany. If you're only visiting one country, then buying a one-country pass will be cheaper than buying a Global pass covering all the countries. If you're only visiting Switzerland, buy a Swiss Travel Pass. If you're only visiting Germany, buy a German Rail Pass.

Some popular trains like the Eurostar, Thalys, TGV, and AVE are included in the Eurail Pass, but require that you purchase a seat reservation. Check out the "Pass network only" feature in the Rail Planner App to see the trains that are included in the Pass.

The Global Pass is valid in all 33 participating countries; as of 2020, they were Austria, Belgium, Bosnia and Herzegovina, Bulgaria, Croatia, Czech Republic, Denmark, Estonia, Finland, France, Germany, Greece, Hungary, Ireland, Italy, Latvia, Lithuania, Luxembourg, Montenegro, the Netherlands, North Macedonia, Norway, Poland, Portugal, Romania, Serbia, Slovakia, Slovenia, Spain, Sweden, Switzerland, Turkey, and the United Kingdom.

A Global Pass fare is dependent on the number of days it is valid in a period of time.

Fare categories are:
    Four, five or seven days in one month (flexi)
    10 or 15 days in two months (flexi)
    15 or 22 continuous days
    One, two or three continuous months

Continuous passes-- unlimited travel every day for a continuous period of time, either 15 days, 22 days or 1, 2 or 3 months, starting on any date you like.

Flexi passes-- 4, 5, 7, 10 or 15 days unlimited travel within an overall 1 or 2 month period. For example, take the 5 days in 1 month pass...The overall 1 month starts ticking on the date you validate your pass at a station, you can then 'spend' each of your 5 days of unlimited travel any time during that 1 month period, on whatever dates you like.

The most convenient way to travel in 33 countries across Europe is to buy the Eurail Global pass. Download the Rail Planner app on your iPhone or Android phone, and buy the pass in the app. The pass will then be available on your phone. You can add journeys to your pass as you go. Buy passes up to 11 months in advance of travel. No need to choose a start date. The pass will start when you enter your first journey and click on "use pass." Eurail will give you a free replacement pass if you lose your phone.

Be aware that prices could vary, but this table will give you a general idea of how much a rail pass costs as of Fall 2020.

Eurail Global pass prices	Standard (2nd) class		1st class	
	Adult (aged 28-59)	Senior (over 60)	Adult (aged 28-59)	Senior (over 60)
4 days in a month	**$342**	$307	$455	$410
5 days in a month	$391	$310	$458	$412
7 days in a month	$408	$368	$543	$488
10 days in a month	$489	$440	$651	$586
15 days in 2 months	$601	$541	$801	$720
15 days continuous	$540	$486	$719	$647
22 days continuous	$631	$568	$841	$757
1 month continuous	$817	$735	$1,088	$980
2 months continuous	$891	$802	$1,188	$1,070
3 months continuous	$1,099	$990	$1,465	$1,318

1st or 2nd class?

2nd class is absolutely fine. Many local trains are 2nd class only. 1st class seating is available on most longer-distance trains. It's nicer with wider, plusher seats, and more legroom. Sometimes 1st class trains carriages serve food, but don't assume that food will be available.

The biggest advantage of 1st class is that there are usually fewer people per car. Sometimes a 1st class pass will get you into a first class lounge at a station, but not usually.

2nd Class Seats on UK train

Paying for reservations

As mentioned earlier, reservation fees may be charged in some countries. Variable price tickets (i.e. high-speed trains and long/medium-distance routes) often require a reservation, and, if you're traveling with a Eurail pass, you'll need to pay extra for the reservation. You can make the reservation online or at the train station ticket window. Many countries (Austria, Denmark, Germany, the UK, and most of Eastern Europe) don't require reservations on their trains. However, it's often possible to book a reservation if you want a guaranteed seat.

Avoiding reservations fees

You might be able to avoid reservation fees by taking slower or less comfortable trains. Multiple trains typically serve a route, so look for trains in the Railplanner app that do not require reservations.

How to make reservations online

There is no central website for all passholder reservations. Different operators use different reservation systems. However, some passholder reservations can be made online, with no added booking fees and simply printed out or collected at the

1st class train travel, Liverpool to London

station. Go to the Eurail reservations page. Select the starting country for your journey. That page will list major train services from that country to neighboring countries, and tell you if journeys can be booked online, and if so where and how.

Making reservations at the station

Show your rail pass at the ticket window, tell the agent where and when you want to travel, and ask for the reservation. Be prepared and write down your request on a piece of paper or as a note on your phone in the local language, just in case the agent doesn't speak English. You can then show your request to the agent and avoid worry about miscommunication due to language issues. In some countries, such as Italy, it's easier to use the self-service touch-screen ticket machines for passholder reservations.

Best countries for using rail passes...

Some countries don't typically require seat reservations, so there are no additional fees for pass holders on regular trains. Ireland, the Netherlands, Belgium, Luxembourg, Germany, Switzerland, Austria, Denmark & most of central & eastern Europe do not require seat reservations, even on longer-distance inter-city trains. You won't have any additional fees, unless you want a reserved seat, couchette, or sleeper on an overnight train.

In these countries, hop on any train without a reservation and sit in any unreserved empty seat. If the train takes reservations, a marquee above the seat will display if it is reserved and from which station. When the conductor asks for tickets, show your pass and the QR code for your ticket on your phone in the Rail Planner app. The conductor will scan the QR code, just like s/he would do if you had a paper ticket. This is the case even on premier high-speed trains, like Germany's superb ICE or Austria's railjet trains. If you make a reservation, you can pick up the ticket stub at the station and show the stub to the conductor.

There are some important exceptions in these countries:

Thalys high-speed trains between Brussels & Amsterdam and between Brussels & Cologne have compulsory reservation and a fee for rail pass holders.

A few scenic tourist trains in Switzerland require a seat reservation and small supplement, such as the Glacier Express & Bernina Express.

Less good countries for using rail passes...

In some countries, pass holders must make a reservation and pay a fee for almost every inter-city journey. Be aware that this will the case even for international journeys ending in these countries.

France
Italy
Sweden
Spain
Portugal

Plan on paying approximately €10 for every train ride. Sometimes it's less, sometimes more, notably a French TGV is either €10 or €20, and Thalys Paris-Brussels-Amsterdam is €15-€25. The upside is that it would have cost you much more without the pass.

Another important limitation is quotas. Some trains have quotas for pass holders, which means these trains will charge you full fare when the pass holder quota is exceeded. Some of these trips include Paris-Brussels-Amsterdam Thalys, Paris-Switzerland TGV-Lyria, Paris-Turin-Milan TGVs & Paris-Barcelona TGVs.

For other trains, including French domestic TGVs and Spanish or Italian high-speed trains, passholders can always get seats unless the train is physically full.

What your Eurail pass does not cover

- City buses, trams & metros in big cities. These public transportation options are usually run by urban transit authorities, not by the national train operator. For unlimited travel, look for options in each destination. For example, buy a Paris Pass from www.raileurope.com if you want unlimited bus & metro travel in Paris for a day or more.
- Private train operators, such as the Euskotren narrow-gauge local trains in Spain, the Circumvesuviana railway Naples-Pompeii-Sorrento

or the Jungfrau line in Switzerland.

- Private operators who now compete with state-owned national train operators, such as Italo high-speed trains in Italy, and GWTR and Arriva in the Czech Republic.

Remember to download the Railplanner App, buy your pass in the app, and keep track of your journeys in the app. If required, buy your reservation through a 3ʳᵈ party vendor or at the train station. When you ride a train, show the conductor your ticket and QR code in the Railplanner app.

Other non-Eurail passes

Sometimes non-Eurail passes are better value than Eurail. The Swiss Travel Pass is the best option if you are only traveling in **Switzerland**, because there is no one-country Eurail pass for that country (www.sbb.ch). **German** Railways (DB) provides the German Pass.

The Renfe **Spain** Pass might be cheaper than the Eurail one-country Spain pass; it's not the same as the Eurail single country Spain pass. Renfe's Spain Pass allows a set number of journeys, not unlimited travel per day. You pay for between 4 and 12 journeys in a one-month period. The Renfe Spain Pass is usually a better deal than the Eurail Spain pass -- reservations are included with no hidden extra reservation costs. In contrast, Eurail holders pay a €6 to €10 reservation fee per journey on almost all long-distance Spanish trains, but it's all included with Renfe's Spain Pass. Plus the Renfe's Spain Pass reservations can be made online. Buy a Renfe's Spain Pass either online at www.renfe.com/EN/viajeros/ viajes_internacionales/spain-pass (no fee, but the system may struggle with some payment cards) or at www.petrabax.com (small mark-up, but it's in plain English with no payment problems). The pass is emailed to you.

Portuguese Rail pass is a good option if you are traveling in **Portugal**. Check Portuguese point-to-point fares at www.cp.pt. Long-distance trains almost always require a reservation. Check details, prices & buy at www.raileurope.com.

BritRail Pass for Britain. Check details, prices & buy at www.raileurope.com. Reservations are never compulsory on British trains, just hop on and show your pass. British point-to-point fares can be found at www.nationalrail.co.uk if you want to comparison shop. If you are using a Eurail pass, it may not trigger the entry gates to the train platforms. We traveled in Spring 2021 with a Eurail Global pass and had to find an attendant every time we needed to enter or exit the platform gates. The Britrail pass will not have that issue.

The Benelux Tourrail pass covers the **Netherlands, Belgium & Luxembourg**. Check details, prices & buy at www.raileurope.com.

The Eastern Europe pass covers **Austria, Hungary, Czech Republic, Slovakia**. Buy this pass at www.acprail.com or www.raileurope.com.

The Balkan Flexipass gives unlimited 1st class travel on the national rail networks in **Bulgaria, Bosnia & Herzegovina, Greece, Montenegro, Republic of Macedonia, Serbia, The Serbian Entity of Bosnia Herzegovina, and Turkey**, with a choice of 5, 10, or 15 days of unlimited train travel in a one-month period. Buy the pass at www.acprail.com or www.raileurope.com. A word of caution...train travel is not as common in some of the eastern European countries. You might have better luck taking a bus or booking a private car & driver.

Summary of your options for buying train tickets

1. Buy a Eurail pass, remembering that a reservation fee must be paid for certain trains;
2. Buy point-to-point tickets as you go- cheap for short trips, expensive for longer distances;
3. Buy cheap advance-purchase tickets direct from the operator with limited or no refunds or changes to travel plans allowed;
4. Mix & match these options: Combine a Eurail pass with regular tickets for short trips or pre-planned longer journeys

Here's a tip...just because you have a pass, it doesn't mean that you have to use it on every trip. If you have a flexi pass for a set number of days, then use those days for longer, more expensive trips. Pay for short, cheap trips. For example, a day trip from Florence to Pisa is about €16 which is less than the value of one day of your pass (approximately €50 per day).

Finding the best train timetable

The Railplanner app has a journey planner that will provide options for routes. There's also a German Railways online timetable that covers national rail operators across Europe... www.bahn.de/en. A downside is that it only provides routes for national operators. In other words, trains operated by Italo, FEVE, Euskotren, Regiojet, Leo Express or the Circumvesuviana and so on, are not included.

Using a pass on overnight trains...

Overnight trains usually have sleeping berths. Couchettes are basic bunks with a blanket & pillow. For retirees, the 4 or 6 per compartment might not be as comfortable as other options (think youth hostel).

Sleeper compartments are hotels on rails, with proper beds & washbasin, 1, 2, 3, or occasionally 4 beds per compartment.

The fee is usually per bed, not per compartment. A couchette costs around €20-€37 in western Europe, perhaps €10-€18 in eastern Europe in a 6-bunk compartment. A bed in a more comfortable sleeper is typically €40-€92 per bed in a 2-berth sleeper in western Europe, €20-€35 in eastern Europe.

If you have a flexi-type pass, an overnight train only uses one day on your pass, the day of departure. Here is the new rule, as of January 2019: A Eurail flexi pass day normally runs from midnight to midnight. But if you board any overnight train before midnight, and do not change trains after midnight, you only need to use one day on a Flexi pass, the day of departure.

Using your rail pass...
Go to the train station (many of them have a dedicated pass holder window) and say; *"I have a Eurail Pass and I want a reservation for the train from "A" to "B" on X day (even possible for the same day) and at X hour."*

If you travel without having entered the trip in the travel report and pass, you risk a fine and payment of a full fare ticket.

There is a limited reservation availability for pass holders, so even if there's space on the train, a ticket agent can tell you there's no space for you with your pass. This is rare unless you're traveling during high season or a very popular route.

If you have a paper pass, your Eurail pass consists of a ticket and a pass cover. Each time before boarding a train, bus or boat, it is important that you record your trip in the "travel report" on the pass cover (in blue or black ink) and write the date of travel on your pass, too.

If you have an electronic pass in the Railplanner app, be sure to save your trip to the pass and click on "use pass" to add the trip to your pass.

If it's an electronic pass, add the trip to the pass on the Rail Planner app prior to travel.

Bus travel

The easiest way to book travel by bus between cities and countries is to use an online travel service, such as https://www.thetrainline.com/buses/europe. Busses are one of the most economical ways to travel, but they aren't as scenic as trains, not as fast, have no restaurant or bar, may not have a toilet, and you must stay in your seat while traveling. Moreover, bringing your own food and drink on board is usually not allowed...definitely, no alcohol.

That said, the bus will get you to small towns and large cities in air-conditioned comfort. Some busses offer WiFi and power sockets. Traveling across borders is easy. Popular trans-European busses, such as Flixbus and Eurolines, operate services across borders in almost all western European countries.

Getting the best price on bus tickets in Europe

Using an online service, such as Trainline, is an easy and efficient way to check and compare fares. Buying fares in advance will usually save you money. Trainline can also tell you when fares are about to increase. Coach tickets go on sale around 3 months before the date of travel. Also, keep an eye out for deals and discounts. Most European bus/coach operators offer standard prices as well as special offers. Discounted tickets are released in advance, but are limited in number. Lower cost fares sell out quickly, so best to act on it if you find a good deal.

Booking buses in Europe

Just like with trains, there are many bus operators in Europe. You can book through an individual operator ticketing system, or use an online travel service (e.g. Trainline). You'll find your available journeys and fares through the online ticketing system. Once you book the ticket, you'll receive an electronic ticket. Show the electronic ticket to the driver as you board the bus.

If you have questions, there are staff at the bus stations who can help you. Consider writing your questions in the local language either on your phone or piece of paper to show to the station attendants. Never assume that everyone (or anyone) will speak English. Always have a note that asks where the toilet is located.

On the day of travel

Plan enough time to arrive at the station, find your terminal and board your coach. The same goes for journeys that require changes. When booking tickets for a non-direct bus journey, select realistic options with enough time to change coaches. Consider that most of the main bus stations in Europe are very large. It could take 10 minutes or so to walk from one terminal to another.

At the station

Just like in train stations, electronic departure boards can be found in most stations' entrance halls. They will show live bus times and terminal information. Know the words for Arrivals and Departures in the local language.

Changes in bus times such as delays and platform changes will be shown on departure boards as well as being announced, usually in the local language and English, via loudspeakers. Platforms are usually numbered continuously, starting with 1. Signage and station maps will lead the way. All the large European train stations are equipped with luggage storage facilities, toilets, shops and restaurants as well as ticket booking offices and information desks.

Main bus companies in Europe

- National Express
- ALSA
- Eurolines
- Flixbus
- Marino
- Marozzi
- Terravision
- Isilines

Bus Operators in Popular Tourist Destinations

UK: A large number of bus and coach operating companies, including National Express, FirstGroup and Stagecoach, provide an extensive network of busses across the UK.

Italy: Baltour is the main operator, as well as Marozzi and Marino

France: Several reliable bus companies serve France, including OUIBUS. International coach companies serve French destinations as well as routes abroad such as Flixbus, Eurolines and Isilines.

Overnight ferry between Split, Croatia and Ancona, Italy

Spain: The main bus operator is ALSA. It covers the entire length of the country. Other popular companies serving various routes in Spain are Avanza and Socibus.

Germany: Operators such as Flixbus and IC Bus are very reliable.

Subways and Trams

Larger cities have subway or tram services. You can usually buy tickets at kiosks adjacent to a stop. When you enter the carriage or tram, you'll need to scan or insert a ticket. You may also need to rescan or insert the ticket at an exit turnstile. It's worth exploring this type of transportation when you visit a city. Ask your front desk or host for information about how to use the subway or trams. See Chapter 7 for a thorough presentation of options for public transportation in London, Paris, and Rome.

Ferries and river boats

First, If you have a Eurail pass, consider using ferries associated with your Eurail Pass. Ferries can be an excellent way to travel between some coastal destinations if the train trip would be quite long. For example, travel between Ancona, Italy and Split, Croatia on an overnight ferry is about 11 hours, whereas a train trip will be approximately 24 hours.

Consider that ferries are often not like nice cruise liners. The berths can be very compact and spartan. However, you do have a bed, toilet, and shower -- even in very tight quarters. Ferries are also a great option for reaching islands (e.g. Santorini, Capri, Hvar). You could take a small plane or helicopter, but the price will be high. Eurail Passes allow access to a number of discounted European ferry routes and boats.

Here is the information from the Eurail site
https://www.eurail.com/en/get-inspired/trains-europe/ferries

"It is often possible to buy discounted ferry tickets in advance. We (Eurail) recommend you purchase these tickets in advance when planning to travel during high season. To make your booking, contact the ferry company directly. In some cases, you can buy the ticket with the discount already included. Occasionally, however, you will have to buy the full fare ticket, and the ferry company will refund the discount.

For free passage on international ferry routes, your pass must be valid for the country of departure and arrival. For discounted passage, your pass must be valid for the country of departure or arrival.

When traveling by night ferry (Superfast, Minoan or Blue Star Ferries) you have to fill in the day of departure in your pass travel calendar. If you are still on this ferry after midnight, you don't have to use a second travel day, unless you board a second ferry.

Below you can find an overview of the major ferry companies that have a partnership with Eurail.

(Spain - Morocco - Algeria) Balearia runs ferries between mainland Spain and its cluster of Spanish Islands (the Balearic Islands). Travel to the scenic gems of the Mediterranean: Mallorca, Menorca, Ibiza, and Formentera. Balearia ferries can also take you across the Mediterannean Sea to northern Africa.

Ferry interior seating -- traveling among Croatian Islands

(Greece) Blue Star Ferries operate on various routes from the Greek mainland to many of its beautiful islands. An exotic destination like Greece calls for a relaxing journey to its pristine beaches and ancient ruins. Equipped with a range of facilities, the convenience and comfort of these ferries will ensure you the journey is all part of your experience.

(Finland - Germany - Sweden) Finnlines operates ferries across the Baltic Sea. With 5-star facilities and top-notch comfort onboard, discover Europe like Europeans do. Shorten your journey time, and gather some new experiences along the way.

(Denmark - Norway - Sweden) Sail from Denmark to several destinations on the shores of Norway and Sweden with Fjord Line ferries.

(Greece - Spain - Italy - Malta) Grimaldi Lines offers a variety of routes to choose from — travel to Greece, Spain, Malta, Italy and its magnificent Island of Sardinia. Admire the spectacular shores of Europe, as you unwind on the deck of the ferries run by Grimaldi Lines. To shorten long journeys between countries, choose this quick and comfortable ferry trip.

(Ireland - France - Great Britain) Irish Ferries operates ferry routes between the Republic of Ireland, France and Wales. Take an offbeat ferry route — explore the Irish panorama and taste the Irish waters.

(Greece - Italy) Minoan Lines offers ferry connections within Greece and between Greece and Italy. While you are enjoying the activities on board, travel swiftly and get more time to explore your desired destination.

(Poland - Sweden - Denmark) Travel by ferry between Poland and destinations on the shores of Sweden and Denmark with Polferries. You can enjoy a variety of entertainment services on board as you sail across the Baltic Sea.

(Italy - Croatia) SNAV Ferries travel across the Adriatic Sea, connecting Italy and Croatia. They also travel between the Italian city of Naples and the Aeolian and Pontine Islands.

(Ireland- Netherlands- Great Britain- Norway- Sweden- Denmark- Germany- Poland- Latvia) Stena Line connects Great Britain (England, Scotland, Wales) with Ireland (Republic of Ireland and Northern Ireland) and the Netherlands. This ferry company provides a great travel option to reach mainland Europe from Great Britain and Ireland. They also have a comprehensive network of ferries sailing the Baltic Sea between Germany, Poland, Norway, Sweden, Denmark and Latvia.

(Greece- Italy) Superfast Ferries travel across the serene Adriatic Sea. Soak up the breathtaking view of the azure waters between Greece and Italy.

(Finland- Sweden- Estonia- Latvia) Explore the Baltic Sea, as Tallink Silja operates ferries between Finland, Sweden and the Åland Islands, as well as the Baltic countries of Estonia and Latvia.

(Sweden- Finland- Estonia) Experience the most beautiful archipelago in the world — a Viking Line cruise is an unforgettable experience! Viking Line offers you a sustainable and comfortable way to travel on the Baltic Sea with a fleet of seven passenger ships operating between Finland, Sweden and Estonia."

See http://www.doitineurope.com/transportation/ferries-by-river.htm for a nice list of river ferries and cruises in Germany, France and England. An excerpt from their website is below:

Rhine River Ferries and Cruises (Germany)
- Bad Breisig-Bad Honningen Ferry
- Bingen-Ruedesheim Ferry
- Boppard-Filsen Ferry
- Kaub-Oberwesel Ferry
- Linz-Remagen Ferry
- Lorch-Niederheimbach Ferry
- Remagen-Erpel Ferry
- St. Goar-St. Goarshausen Ferry
RHINE RIVER DAY CRUISES
- Bingen-Ruedesheimer Rhine Day Cruises
- Bonn BSP

- KD Rhine River Day Cruises
- Loreley Line Rhine Day Cruises
- Primus Frankfurt
- Roessler Assmannshausen

MULTIPLE DAY RHINE RIVER CRUISES
- AMA Waterways: European Rivers
- Avalon Waterways: Rhine River Cruises
- Cosmos Rhine River Cruises
- Viking River Cruises: European Rivers

RHINE RIVER CASTLES
- Liebenstein Castle / Burg Liebenstein
- Marksburg Castle / Marksburg Fortress
- Mouse Castle / Berg Maus
- Rheinfels Castle / Burg Rheinfels
- Stolzenfels Castle / Schloss Stolzenfels

OTHER RHINE RIVER ATTRACTIONS
- Rhine Gorge (UNESCO World Heritage Site)
- Cologne Cathedral (Roman Catholic Church in Cologne)
- Lorelei Rock (near St. Goarshausen Town)

Seine River Ferries and Cruises (France)

Bateau Mouches

Bateaux Parisiens

Vedettes du Pont-Neuf

Batobus Water Bus

Thames River Ferries (England UK)

Thames Clippers

Westminster Passenger Service Association

Tate-to-Tate Gallery Boat

Thames River Services

Woolwich Free Ferry

Dinner Cruises on the Thames River
- Bateaux London Dinner Cruise
- City Cruises: Showboat Dinner Cruise

Charter Cruises on the Thames River
- Silver Fleet Charters
- Thames Executive Charters

Hiring a car and driver or renting a car

Hiring or renting cars might be the most expensive and/or difficult strategy for traveling around Europe. Sometimes, there isn't another good option to get where you want to go. In that case, we would probably hire a private tour guide or take a small group tour.

In general, cars are only allowed in historic city centers with a special permit. You will be fined if you accidentally drive in the city center without a permit. It will be very difficult to find a parking space; parking spaces are rare. Driving within the cities and towns will be crowded so plan on navigating difficult traffic.

Even if you take a private guided tour, the driver will drop you off near the city center or park in designated parking outside of the city center and walk in with you. If you're visiting cities or more populated towns, consider using the public transportation. Busses are relatively easy to use and very inexpensive.

There are some instances where renting a car could be a great idea, like driving through the Dordogne in France. Get on your computer and do some research on the region before deciding to rent a car. If other travelers report good experiences, then go for it.

Keep in mind that you'll need to obtain an international driver license (IDL) before you leave the US. It is issued in conjunction with your US driver license. You can get an IDL through AAA while you're still in the US. See the AAA website for the most up to date information (https://www.aaa.com/vacation/idpf.html).

To apply for an IDL, submit the following to AAA:

- Your completed IDP application form
- Two original passport pictures each signed on the back
- $20 USD permit fee

- A photocopy of both sides of your driver's license
- If desired, include additional U.S. funds for expedited return mail service. See USPS.com Fedex.com or UPS.com f

Renting cars is different than renting in the US. Read all the fine print very carefully. Ask for a car with an updated GPS system that will give you directions and notifications in English. Also, rental car companies in Europe may not let you cross country borders, regardless of whether the country is in the EU or Schengen Area. You might be charged cost prohibitive fees for one-way cross-border rentals.

Hiring a private driver is a very good option for travel in some areas, especially eastern Europe, where the prices are lower than other places in Europe. While traveling during the Pandemic, we used private drivers in Serbia and Croatia and felt that it was well worth the money. In addition to taking you to sight-seeing places, the drivers may also help you find local restaurants, medical clinics, salons and spas, etc. Our driver in Croatia drove us from Split to Cavtat (south of Dubrovnik) and then picked us up a week later and returned us to Split. It was the absolute best way – least expensive, fast, and no hassle-- to manage that trip. To make the drive, we had to pass through Bosnia-Hercegovina, which meant clearing border patrol entering and exiting. We think it's always nice to be with a local, native speaker when crossing borders if we're not on public transportation.

To find a driver, start by asking your apartment host or hotel front desk. Next, use Google or another search engine to find "private tour guides near me." Read the reviews on the tour guides. Send them an email and ask if they speak English, type of vehicle, and fees for private tours or transport. Provide a brief description of what you would like to do.

CHAPTER 7:
USING PUBLIC TRANSPORTATION IN EUROPEAN HUBS: LONDON, PARIS, AND ROME

Chapter 7: Using Public Transportation in European Hubs: London, Paris, and Rome

London

Subway (The Tube), Busses, Trams, and Overground

Riding public transportation in London is fairly easy. Buy an Oyster card at one of the underground (tube) stations. If there is no ticket window, then use a machine. Cash or credit cards are accepted.

The Oyster card costs 5 pounds, and you might start by adding 20 pounds to the card. Each time you ride the tube or a bus, tap the contactless Oyster card on the payment machine. The amount of the fare/ticket will be deducted from your balance. Add more pounds as needed. Machines are located in all underground stations. You'll need to use your Oyster card to enter and leave most tube stations. Be prepared to tap your card to exit the turnstile.

An Oyster card allows you to travel between all parts of London on the Underground, Trams (DLR), Overground, some river boats, and the iconic red London buses. As a general rule a Travelcard is more expensive than an Oyster card or Contactless payment card. The exception is if you make 3 or more journeys for 6 days or more within a 7 day period. For unlimited travel on the tube, you can buy a London Underground pass for 3 or 7 days. It's called a London Visitor Travelcard and can be bought in London at an Underground station.

London Eye

Oyster cards are electronic smartcards that are used to pay for public transport in London.

Visitor Oyster cards, Oyster cards and contactless payment cards are the cheapest way to travel in London.

To use an Oyster card, touch the card on the yellow reader at the gates as you enter and end your journey. You don't need to touch out at the end of your journey on buses and trams.

You can buy a Visitor Oyster card online before you arrive in London, or Oyster cards at TfL Visitor Centres, stations and Oyster ticket shops.

To travel from the airport into London, you have several options. The following site provides information to help you decide which option is best for you if you are traveling from Gatwick: London - Gatwick Airport train cheaper than Gatwick Express. Here is a comparable site for Heathrow airport:

London Heathrow Airport - Practical Information On Using Heathrow Including Comprehensive Transfer Comparisons. It's easy to take the train from Gatwick or Heathrow into London.

Trains

If you have a Eurail pass that includes England, you can use the pass to ride the train into London from the airport. Make sure it is validated before boarding the train (check at a ticket window). Also, be sure to write down the date, train time, and destination in your journey log. Some countries regularly check your log as well as your pass and passport. If you have an electronic pass, then save the journey in your RailPlanner app. Then click on the "Use a day" option.

The RailPlanner app will help you find ways to travel between stations, including using busses. It's always a good idea to check with the ticket agent at the train station when planning a train trip. We found that the app doesn't always take into consideration bank holidays and interruptions to rail service. For example, one day, the tracks were flooded and rail busses were taking passengers from station to station. On another day, a bank holiday meant cancellation of a number of routes. We took two different busses, but it wasn't timely and we missed our train from Manchester Piccadilly to Cardiff Central. We ended up taking an Uber (very expensive!). Lesson learned – always have a back-up plan and be prepared to go with the flow when public transportation mishaps occur.

Taxis

London's official taxis, black cabs can be hailed in the street or at designated ranks situated in prominent places, including many mainline rail, Tube and bus stations. They can also be booked by telephone. Only black cabs can be hailed in the street. If the yellow TAXI sign is on, the cab is available for hire. Black cabs are metered and there is a minimum charge of £3.20 ($4.52). Additional charges apply when you take a black cab from Heathrow, book by telephone, and on Christmas Day and New Year's Eve. All black cabs accept payment by credit or debit card, and there is no surcharge on the taxi fare for card payment. Tips are not expected, but are appreciated. Most people round up to the nearest pound.

Iconic London phone booth

If the yellow TAXI sign at the front is illuminated, the cab is available for hire. Black cabs are legally obliged to take on any job for journeys up to 12 miles (20 miles for cabs at the Heathrow Airport taxi ranks), or up to one-hour duration.

Another option is private hire vehicles, which range from local minicab companies to chauffeur driven limousines. Minicabs can be a cheaper alternative- ask prices beforehand as they are not on a meter.

Only book a licensed minicab with a Transport for London license disc. Unbooked minicabs are illegal, unsafe and uninsured. You may be approached by minicab drivers seeking passengers or offering a service; avoid accepting these solicitations. The rides are unsafe, unlicensed, uninsured and illegal. You can check with Transport for London to see if an operator is licensed.

If you want to book a private hire vehicle or minicab by telephone, most hotels and hostels will have a list of reputable, licensed operators. You will also find minicab offices on most high (like our Main streets in the US) streets. All licensed private hire vehicles have a distinctive Transport for London license disc in the front and rear windscreen.

Bicycling

You can hire bikes using London's public cycle hire, Santander Cycles. There are more than 750 docking stations and 11,500 bikes to hire around London. It costs £2 ($2.82) to access a Santander Cycles bike for 24 hours; the first 30 minutes of each journey are free. For longer journeys, it costs an extra £2 for each additional 30 minutes.

Bikes can be hired using a bank card at the docking station or using the official app. To use a bike, find a bike station and pay the fee, ride it where you like, then return it to any of the hundreds of docking stations across the city.

Avoid simply parking a bike while you sightsee. Instead, return it to a docking station. When you're ready to ride again, get another bike.

You can also use your phone to help you use a bike. The official Santander Cycles app, available on iPhone and on Android, is the only app to send bike-release codes straight to your phone. Use the app and skip past the docking-station terminal and get on your bike more quickly.

Download the Santander Cycles app and register for pay-as-you-pedal. Use the app to "hire now" from a nearby docking station and get your release

111

code. Tap your code into the docking point and start cycling. The app will also provide up-to-the-minute information about which docking stations have bikes and spaces available. You can use it to plan a journey with an easy-to-follow map. The app can provide notifications with the cost at the end of your journey. Check the app to see your recent journeys and charges.

Paris

One option for using public transportation is the Paris Visite Metro Pass. There are 5 zones (1-5). Depending on which zones you choose, Paris Visite allows you to travel on the metro, RER, Transilien suburban train networks, tramway, bus (except the Jetbus, Allobus, Roissy CDG, tourist bus routes and Air France buses), Orlyval, and the Montmartre funicular.

Paris Visite also provides discounts at various museums and sites. The pass is valid for 1, 2, 3 or 5 consecutive days for a price ranging from €11.65 to €63.90. Purchase your Paris Visite travel pass from ticket desks or automatic vending machines.

You can also book online with Parisinfo. Select your Paris Visite travel pass and pick up at a ticket desk. Each ticket or travel pass (whether for a day, a week, or a month) is valid for designated zones.

Eiffel Tower

The zone system might seem a little confusing. The zones are concentric: zones 1-3 include downtown Paris and the closest urban areas, while zones 4 and 5 cover more distant areas, including Versailles and Disneyland Paris®.

Two exceptions are worth noting:

All Paris metro stations are accessible with a ticket or travel pass that covers only zones 1 and 2, even though some are located geographically in zone 3: for example, you can take the metro to La Défense Grande Arche (zone 3) with a t+ ticket. On the other hand, if you take the RER or a bus, you will need to purchase a ticket that specifies your destination.

Orlyval, the light train line between the Antony RER station and Orly Airport, has a specific fare.

Check the options that best meet your needs and circumstances at https://www.ratp.fr/en/titres-et-tarifs/paris-visite-travel-pass and https://www.ratp.fr/en/visite-paris/english/preparing-your-trip-tickets-and-travel-passes-designed-you .

You can buy individual metro tickets at any metro station. Buy tickets from an agent at a ticket window or at a ticket kiosk. Metro tickets and passes can be used on the Metro, on city buses, on the trams that operate on the edges of the city, and on the RER (the deep underground commuter trains) within the central city. It's cheapest to buy a pack of 10 tickets.

Remember to hold on to your ticket each time you enter the Metro. You'll need to use that same ticket to exit the Metro when you arrive at your destination station.

A comprehensive city pass might actually be the best way to maximize your Paris experience. See their website: https://www.parisinsidersguide.com/paris-pass.html

1. Entrance fees to almost all the museums are included.
2. Get priority access entry to museums (e.g. skip the line).
3. Ride the metro for free.
4. Save money if you use it to visit museums and use public transportation each day.
5. Entry to the Palace of Versailles with skip-the-line access.
6. Free River Seine cruise.
7. Hop-on-Hop-off bus tour
8. Helps you discover the smaller, more intimate museums in Paris (free entry).
9. You can cancel up to three days before your pass begins if you change your mind.

Prices vary, but they range from about 128 euros for a 2-day pass to 169 euros for a 4-day pass per adult. That's about $155 to $205. If you're not planning on seeing a lot of sites or using the public transportation, then it might not be worth the investment. We like it because it allows for hassle free travel to all of the major sites. It's great to be able to jump on public transportation without having to stop to buy a ticket at a kiosk or ticket window!

Subway (The Metropolitan) and RER (rapid transit train service)

The Paris metro is operated by RATP and is made up of 16 lines. It's the most common way to get around Paris. The metro lines are numbered and indicated by different colors on the metro map. Look at the metro station where you want to board and then identify the starting and ending destination of available lines to know which line you want to ride.

A single metro ticket costs €1.90, and can be used for one journey, including all connections. White-colored tickets can be purchased singly or in a book of 10 ("carnet") for €16, at the ticket offices or machines in metro stations, and also in some tobacconists.

Put your ticket in the slot at the station turnstile and collect it once it has processed and before walking through the turnstile. You'll need to use the same ticket to exit the metro station at your destination. If you're using a pass, tap it on the pad.

The RER has RATP and SNCF lines A, B, C, D, and E. It serves Paris and the surrounding region. You may use the "ticket T+" on the metro or the RER. The time limits are 90 minutes from entry to exit on the metro, busses, and trams, and 2 hours from entry to exit on the trains.

Be aware that the Eurail pass doesn't work on the regional and city (RER) trains in Paris. Buying metro, bus, and boat tickets as you go could be the most economical.

Busses

Paris is a relatively compact city, so using your own two feet along with low-cost public transportation is definitely the best way of getting around in Paris. There are 58 bus lines in Paris. Bus lines are numbered. Go online and identify the bus lines that will take you where you want to go. Here is a link to the interactive bus map https://www.ratp.fr/en/plans-lignes/plan-des-bus

During the pandemic, the bus company has not been handing out printed bus schedules. Be sure to check the bus routes and pick-up points prior to leaving your lodging, if you don't have access to the Internet while roaming around the city. We found that our cellular service doesn't work well in Europe, and it's best to identify our routes and transportation by connecting to WiFi prior to leaving our lodging.

Buses operate from Monday to Saturday, 7am to 8.30pm. Some lines operate in the evening between 8.30pm and 12.30am, in particular those departing from stations or which serve major metro/RER interchanges, as well as the 3 outer PC lines. Busses availability is limited on Sundays and public holidays.

The bus line number and direction are indicated at the front and on the sides of the bus. You have to ask the driver to stop the bus when you want to get off. At each stop, there is a glass cover or a pole with bus numbers and directions as well as the other bus lines that run there. Electronic signs indicate time until next bus and where the busses are going.

Be sure to get on the bus at the front of the bus and get off the bus at the middle or back. Remember to punch your ticket or validate your pass. Press the red button to request a stop. The "stop requested" light will appear at the front of the bus. To get off the bus, push the button next to the door.

Be aware that the bus schedule at night time is different than during the day. Look for the schedule for the Noctilien (night bus).

The Hop on/Hop off bus is an option, but might not meet your needs. A deluxe 2-day ticket is about €50 ($60) per person. On one line, the sites are hop off only. It's more expensive than just taking the metro or a bus to the sites.

Trams

The trams in Paris completely disappeared in 1957, but were re-introduced in the 1990s by the RATP company. Trams are comfortable, use clean energy, and are inexpensive. The trams are more frequently used by locals than tourists. The lines only run in the city's outskirts...not to many interesting sites. The best tram line for tourists could be line 1-- final destination is Basilica of Saint Denis-- but you can also take the Paris metro line 13 to get to the Basilica.

There are currently seven tram lines in Paris:

T1: Connects Saint-Denis with Noisy-le-Sec in the north of the city.
T2: Connects La Défense with Porte de Versailles in the south.
T3: Links Pont du Garigliano (a RER station) with the metro station Porte d'Ivry.
T5: Runs between Marché de Saint-Denis and Garges-Sarcelles.
T6: Connects Châtillon – Montrouge with Vélizy-Villacoublay
T7: Runs between Villejuif – Louis Aragon and Athis-Mons.
T8: Connects Saint-Denis- Porte de Paris with Épinay – Orgemont.

Paris plans on introducing 2 new tramway lines, T9 and T10, soon.

Uber vs Taxis in Paris

We had mixed experiences with using Uber and taxis in Paris. Here are five of our trips to give you an idea of the different fares we paid.

1. We queued at the airport for a taxi, and our ride was a very nice, spacious sedan. The driver said it was a fixed price fare from Charles de Gaulle airport to Paris city center...54 euros.

On our next trip, we called a taxi company and asked for a taxi to pick us up in about ½ an hour. It was a Saturday morning, and we were traveling from our apartment near the Louvre to the Moulin Rouge in Montmartre to meet a tour group. It was about a 2 mile distance by car...1.9 miles by foot.

The driver took a circuitous route, taking about 20 minutes with no traffic to get to our destination. The meter said 10.80 euros when we arrived. He clicked a button and it became 17.80 euros. We paid the fare, but it seemed excessive. Back at our apartment, the front desk explained that a surcharge is added when you prebook a taxi, thus the extra 7 euros.

2. Next, we decided to use Uber after feeling ripped off by the taxi. We booked an Uber from our apartment near the Louvre to the Roland Garros tennis garden. It was about 8 miles away. The cost was 30.80 euros.

3. Upon leaving the tennis tournament, we found a taxi on the street – a very nice, large BMW. The driver said it would cost between 12 and 20 euros to take us back to the Louvre, depending on Tuesday afternoon traffic. We arrived at the Louvre in about 20 minutes; the meter read 13.80 euros.

We felt like this taxi ride was a much better deal, given that we traveled the same distance as in the Uber.

4. The next morning (Wednesday), we booked a taxi to the airport, but this time I asked about the fare in advance. She said it was 57 euros fixed price. When we arrived at the airport, the driver said the fare was 60 euros. We didn't argue with him, because we would have tipped more than the extra he was charging.

We left Paris not knowing if it was better to take a taxi or an Uber. The lowest fare was for the taxi that we found at a taxi stand for an immediate ride. Our best advice is to ask the cost of the fare prior to committing to the ride.

Bicycling

The cheapest, but especially most efficient way of transport to get around Paris is the Velib, the Paris City Council self-service bicycles. You pay a fee of 1,70 euros for a day ticket or 8 euros for a week ticket. During the validity of this ticket you can use any bicycle from the Velib network. We saw many people riding bicycles and electric scooters on our visit in May 2021. Bike lanes are plentiful in central Paris.

Rome

One very cheap ticket or transport card allows you to use almost all means of public transport in Rome with the exception of taxis and airport transport. Buses, subway trains, trams (streetcars), and light rail are operated by the same company called ATAC. You can use any of their transport with the same ticket.

One-way ticket (BIT): The BIT ticket lasts 75 minutes from its first validation and allows unlimited transfers between the metro, buses, trams and urban trains. The only transfer that is not allowed is to leave the metro and return (by the metro turnstiles), even if it's within the 75 minutes of validity. The ticket costs € 1.50.

Rome Colosseum

Day pass (BIG): The BIG ticket allows unlimited public transportation from the moment the ticket is validated until midnight of the same day. The BIG day travel card costs € 6.

3-Day Tourist Pass (BTI): The three-day tourist pass (BTI) gives visitors unlimited use of the public transportation from the moment it is first validated and for the following two days. The BTI has a price of € 16.50.

Week pass (CIS): Identical to the BTI card, but valid for seven days instead of three. This travel card costs € 24.

Other travel cards: If you're planning on staying in Rome for a longer period, there are also annual and monthly travel cards.

Public transportation cards include all of the following:

- Metro
- Buses
- Trams
- Cotral bus services (within Rome)
- Urban trains: Rome–Lido, Rome–Viterbo and Rome–Pantano.
- Trenitalia Regional trains

(second class).

Cards and tickets can be bought in vending machines in any metro station, at convenience stores or from newsagents.

Metro

Rome subway stations are marked with red M signs. The Metro comprises

three lines – A (orange), B (blue) and C (green) – which operate on 60 km (37 mi) of route, serving 73 stations. The subway system does not directly extend out to either Fiumicino or Ciampino Airports, but you can make connections to the commuter trains that do.

The system is really 2 main subway lines, A + B. The C line is partially finished, and it is not yet connected to either A or B and is of little use for most visitors to Rome. Part of the reason why the C line is still unfinished due to the potential for future archeology sites along the route.

Interior of Rome Colosseum

Although not very extensive, the subway system is very inexpensive, €1.50 per ride on a single ticket, and these tickets can also be used on buses, trams, and commuter trains within the city, as well.

Busses

Depending on where you are staying and what you want to see, you might find that taking the bus is more practical than taking the subway. The subway doesn't run through much of Rome's historic center and buses, including smaller electric buses, are the only mass transit options available.

Currently, Rome has 338 bus lines that run throughout the day, 22 night buses and 8,260 stops. As traffic is an important issue in Rome, do not get impatient if the buses are delayed or if you get stuck in traffic jams, as it is most likely to happen and at any time of day.

It can be a bit confusing to find the right bus. Since the metro lines of Rome are limited, visitors will most likely need the bus public transport system to get to certain parts of the city. It may not be the most comfortable or punctual form of transportation. Nevertheless, to get to certain monuments and museums it is essential to use the bus.

Many bus stops now include screens with the number of the bus and when the next is due to arrive. Bus tickets can be bought in any metro station, news-stand or convenience stores. If you are planning on using the bus regularly, buy a few at a time or get a travel card, which might be a better option. Always validate your ticket when you get on the bus. It might seem like people in Rome are not validating tickets, but they may have monthly passes which don't have to be inserted into a machine. However, tourists must insert their tickets in a validation machine.

Trams

Rome's trams are usually cleaner than the buses, but the tram lines are small, and the network doesn't get to the city center which makes it less appealing for visitors. Trams run from 5:30 am until midnight every day, like the city buses in Rome.

At night, the trams are replaced by night buses. Remember when you get on any tram to validate your ticket at their validation machines, otherwise you will be fined.

- Line 2: Piazza Mancini – Piazzale Flaminio.
- Line 3: Piazza Thorwaldsen – Trastevere.
- Line 5: Giovanni Amendola – Piazza dei Gerani.
- Line 8: Torre Argentina – Trastevere.
- Line 14: Giovanni Amendola – Palmiro Togliatti.
- Line 19: Piazza Risorgimento – Piazza dei Gerani.

None of these lines has any special attraction for tourists. The best line for travelers is perhaps number 8, which links Trastevere with Largo di Torre Argentina.

Urban railway lines

Urban trains run approximately from 5:30 am to 10:30 pm. The Rome-Lido line runs until later, till 11:30 pm. Trains leave every 10 to 20 minutes, depending on the time of day. The Ferrovie Urbane is made up of following three lines:

- Rome – Lido.
- Rome – Viterbo.
- Rome – Giardinetti.

Of these lines the most important from a tourist's point of view is the Rome-Lido, since it stops at Ostia Antica (If you aren't going to visit Pompeii or Herculaneum, then Ostia Antica is an archaeological site well worth visiting. You can imagine how the city's inhabitants lived centuries ago. It is less impressive and less well preserved than Pompeii or Herculaneum, but interesting, nonetheless).

The tickets are the same as other forms of public transportation in Rome, and can be bought in urban train stations, metro stations, news agents and convenience stores. If your hotel is near one of these stations or you think you'll be using the public transport in Rome regularly, then buy a few tickets at a time or buy a travel card. Keep in mind that if you want to travel to the outskirts, you will have to buy another more expensive ticket.

Taxis

Beware of taxis in Rome. Tourists and locals alike are frequently overcharged. Moreover, taxi rates in Rome are considered quite high compared with other European capital cities.

Estimates of taxi rates are as follows:
- Minimum fare on weekdays from 6 am – 10 pm: € 3
- Minimum fare on public holidays 6 am – 10 pm: € 4.50
- Minimum fare at night time: € 6.50
- Rate per kilometre (Tariff 1): € 1.10
- Rate per kilometre (Tariff 2): € 1.30
- Rate per kilometre (Tariff 3): € 1.60
- Surcharge for each additional suitcase (one per passenger included in the price): € 1

- Surcharge for telephone reservations: € 3.50
- One hour waiting time: € 27

Based on the official taxi rates, an average journey in the center of Rome should cost between 6 and 8 euros. Avoid being swindled by the taxi drivers.

There are official rates to and from both airports: To get to and from Fiumicino Airport and Ciampino Airport will always cost you the same. The journey to/ from Fiumicino costs € 48 and Ciampino, € 30. These prices are valid for up to four passengers and their suitcases. Refuse to pay if you are charged extra.

If at any point you think you are being swindled, don't let the taxi driver intimidate you. Call the Carabinieri to assist you. Also, always ask for a receipt and complain to the taxi company if you think you were overcharged.

The rates from Termini railway station to the city center should cost between € 8 and € 15. If you can, it is always a good idea to check the route on Google Maps before you get in the taxi so you have an idea of how long it takes.

Be sure to choose the correct type of taxi. All taxis in Rome are white, with a taxi roof sign and a taximeter visible at the front of the car. Hail cabs that have a telephone number written on the sides of the vehicle, which means that they work for a taxi company. If you have any problem, write down the taxi's license plate number (it is always at the back of the front seats) and call the taxi company.

Taxi companies

Although the cheapest way to catch a cab is by waiting at the official taxi stops on the streets of Rome, it is also possible to reserve this type of transportation by telephone. These are some of the best taxi companies in the city:

Radio Taxi: 06-3570.
Pronto Taxi: 06-6645.
Other companies: 06-5551, 06-4994, 06-4157.

CHAPTER 8:
THINGS TO KNOW ABOUT MONEY WHILE TRAVELING IN EUROPE

Chapter 8: Things to know about Money While Traveling in Europe

- European countries and currencies
- Tips for obtaining local currency at the best rate
- Typical needs for cash in Europe
- Credit cards and foreign transaction fees
- Contactless cards
- Using an ATM to get local currency
- Disputing debit card charges?
- Choosing a good credit card for European travel
- Choosing your checking account bank
- Summary tips for obtaining cash and using credit cards while traveling
- Buying through Amazon while in Europe

Venice, Italy

European countries, of course, do not use the US dollar as currency. The Euro is the official currency in many European countries (the Eurozone). Be aware of the currency for your destination prior to setting out on your travels. Keep in mind that a country may be a member of the EU, but not a member of the Eurozone.

European Countries and Currencies (February 2021)

Country	Currency
Austria (EU)	Euro
Albania	Albanian Lek
Andora	Euro
Armenia	Armenian Dram
Azerbaijan	Azerbaijani Manat
Belarus	Belarusian Ruble
Belgium (EU)	Euro
Bosnia & Herzegovina	Bosnia & Herzegovina convertible mark
Bulgaria (EU)	Bulgarian Lev
Croatia (EU)	Croatian Kuna
Cyprus (EU)	Euro
Czechia (EU)	Czech Koruna
Denmark (EU)	Danish Krone
Estonia (EU)	Euro
Finland (EU)	Euro
France (EU)	Euro
Georgia	Georgian Lari
Germany (EU)	Euro
Greece (EU)	Euro
Hungary (EU)	Hungarian Forint
Iceland	Icelandic Krona
Ireland (EU)	Euro
Italy (EU)	Euro
Kosovo	Euro
Latvia (EU)	Euro
Liechtenstein	Swiss Franc
Lithuania (EU)	Euro
Luxembourg (EU)	Euro
Malta (EU)	Euro
Moldova	Moldovan Leu
Monaco	Euro
Montenegro	Euro
Netherlands (EU)	Euro
North Macedonia	Second Macedonian Denar
Norway	Norwegian Krone
Poland (EU)	Polish Zloty
Portugal (EU)	Euro
Romania (EU)	Romanian Leu

Country	Currency
Russia	Russian Ruble
San Marino	Euro
Serbia	Serbian Dinar
Slovakia (EU)	Euro
Slovenia (EU)	Euro
Spain (EU)	Euro
Sweden (EU)	Swedish Krona
Switzerland	Swiss Franc
Turkey	Turkish Lira
Ukraine	Ukrainian Hryvnia
The United Kingdom	Pound Sterling
Vatican City	Euro

Consult this site for updates: https://en.wikipedia.org/wiki/List_of_currencies_in_Europe

Tips for obtaining local currency at the best rate

Here are some terms to understand before you use ATMS or your credit cards when abroad:

**Ponta del Gada,
The Azores, Portugal**

A conversion fee is for the "service" of taking your US dollars and converting them to the local currency. These fees are in addition to variations that a bank or merchant may use in "exchanging" your money. If you have a choice, let your bank or credit card company do the conversion for you.

Exchange rates are the amount of currency that you can "exchange" for another, and rates may vary across establishments and banks.

Foreign transaction fees are charged by credit cards, debit cards, or ATMS and are charges for the service of converting your US dollars to local currency. Make sure you have credit cards with no foreign transaction fees.

You have options for obtaining foreign currency (i.e. cash) in Europe. Here are some tips to help you get cash with the best currency conversion rates and the lowest fees.

1. Several weeks before you leave, you may order foreign currency through your bank or AAA. We tried this method a couple of years ago when we were traveling to the UK. We ordered British Sterling (pounds) from our bank and found that:

The exchange rate was not as good as when we used an ATM in the UK.

The bills were almost all 50 pound notes or higher and many restaurants and shops would not take the larger denominations. Moreover, when we tried to get smaller notes at a bank, they told us that we had to be a customer of the bank to get change. They suggested we try the post office, which we did. The post office told us that they would not provide change for large notes. Finally, we decided to use the large notes to pay our hotel bill. After getting rid of the large notes, we used an ATM to get cash in smaller denominations.

In addition, a UK shop owner told us that the smaller denomination bills that we received from our US bank were "old" currency. That was shocking to us. We thought money was money, but obviously not everywhere. Luckily, we were able to exchange those notes at a UK bank. We're still not sure what the problem was with the notes, but the UK bank did let us exchange our old small denomination notes for new ones.

Lesson learned, ordering from your bank in advance of your trip might not be the best option for obtaining foreign currency.

2. Once you arrive in the country, use an ATM to get cash. If you absolutely must have some cash as soon as you land, then get a small amount (e.g. 100 euros) in the airport from an ATM machine. You can usually find one

in the baggage claim area prior to clearing customs or in the public transportation hall prior to departing the airport. In general, you should be able to travel into the city or town using your credit card to buy a train, bus, or shuttle ticket or to pay for a taxi.

Once you are in your city or town, look for a bank ATM that is in your bank's debit card network. If you use an out-of-network ATM, you'll be charged extra fees and the exchange rate might not be as good as a network bank.

As you're completing your transaction, do NOT choose the option on the screen that allows the ATM bank to "convert" your currency. Recently, we used an ATM in Cambridge, England to get 250 pounds in cash. The ATM indicated that our account would be debited $375 if we chose to let the ATM bank do the conversion to dollars. I chose the option to let my bank do the conversion. When I checked my account, the ATM debit amount was $344. I saved $31 by letting my bank do the conversion.

DO NOT USE THE CURRENCY EXCHANGE COUNTERS IN THE AIRPORT OR TOWN. The exchange rate will not be as good as a network ATM, and the kiosk exchange service may add on fees (as much as 5%).

Last year in Italy, we found that Deutsch Bank provided the best exchange rate and no fees when we used our Capital One 360 debit card. Before you confirm that you want to proceed with a withdrawal, pay careful attention to notices that say a charge is associated with the transaction. If there are fees, consider canceling the transaction and moving on to another bank-affiliated ATM machine.

We highly recommend that you have a checking account and debit card from a bank that does not charge foreign transaction fees. If foreign transaction fees are charged, they may be a percentage of the cash you're withdrawing (up to 5%) or a set fee (e.g. $3.50). In addition, you may be charged fees by your bank AND by the owner of the ATM.

Do NOT use credit cards to get cash from ATM machines. Your credit card company will most likely charge you a high rate of interest beginning the day you withdraw the cash.

3. Lastly, bring foreign currency that you saved from a prior trip. If you're traveling for the first time, this won't be helpful for your arrival in Europe, but keep this option in mind when you're heading back home. You may be tempted to empty your cash into the big bowls in the airport asking you to donate your unused cash to local charities. The flight attendants may also ask you to donate your left-over cash. Be sure to plan for these donations, if you'd like, and then travel back home with at least 100 euros, pounds, or other local currency. We keep currency in our lock box at home for a number of different countries that we intend to visit again. You'll be ready to hit the ground running when you return to the country, and you won't need to worry about finding an ATM right away.

Typical Needs for Cash in Europe

Stow-on-the-Wold, Cotswolds, England

Checking in to your accommodations in Europe: You might need to pay a tourism tax (in cash) when you check-in to your accommodations. Be sure to have enough local currency for this transaction. Your reservation confirmation will usually indicate how much will be due in taxes upon check-in, usually noted as an amount per day. You'll need to do the math (multiply the amount of tax by the number of days of your stay). Your host or front desk clerk will ask you to pay the tax as you're checking in and while they're making a copy of your passport.

Paying for taxis: Not all taxis accept credit cards. Be prepared with enough cash to pay for a ride from the airport to your hotel, especially if you're arriving late at night. You can use the Internet to look up estimates for taxi fare prior to leaving for your trip. Also, some countries have Uber, but not all European countries. In some countries, ride shares are actually illegal.

The best strategy is to have your lodging host make arrangements for your ride from the airport to your hotel or apartment. Oftentimes, this fee can be added to your lodging bill; however, you may be asked to pay the transportation fee along with the local taxes when you check in. Be prepared to tip the driver in cash...10% is plenty. Tipping is not as routine in Europe as in the US, and we have found that it's usually not possible to add a tip to credit card charges.

Making purchases in small shops: You may find that smaller local businesses do not accept credit cards. Always pay **in local currency**, as opposed to euros or dollars. The shop owners may take euros or even US dollars, but be careful of the conversion rate and possible fees that the shop owners might charge when accepting non-local currency.

Tipping in restaurants, taxis, hotels, etc. Tipping is not necessarily expected in Europe, but it is a hard habit for us to break as Americans. The merchant will not have the option to add a tip to your credit card payment, so you'll need to tip in cash. If you're paying with cash, just round up to the nearest euro. We usually tip 10-15% or sometimes more if the price is exceedingly low. For example, in Belgrade, a taxi drove us approxi-

mately 8 miles through the city to a park. The fare was the equivalent of about $7; we gave the driver the equivalent of $10 in Serbian dinars. That same drive in the US would easily have cost $20 or more.

Choosing Credit and Debit Cards for your European Travels

If you aren't mindful, foreign transaction and currency conversion fees can really add up. We experienced a costly lesson in England a few years ago. We used our JP Morgan Chase credit and debit cards over the course of our 3-week vacation. Those cards had fees associated with each use. We spent almost $300 in unnecessary fees during that trip that could have been avoided if we had done some research in advance for cards that were free of foreign transaction fees.

When deciding which credit cards to use in Europe, learn about your existing credit and debit cards first. Call the customer service number on the back of the card, and ask if you will be charged foreign transaction fees with your card. Banks offer so many different credit card options nowadays that it's important to ask about the specific card that

you are carrying. While you are on the phone with them, let them know that you'll be traveling internationally. If your credit card has foreign transaction fees, consider getting a new card with no foreign transaction fees.

Contactless cards

Many establishments and transportation services use contactless payment in Europe. You may have credit or debit cards with a chip, but it might not be a contactless chip. Look at your card to see if it has a contactless symbol.

Cards with contactless chips emit short-range radio waves. When you place your card within a few inches of a contactless-enabled payment terminal, your payment information is transferred. You may be told to tap the terminal, but no tapping is actually needed. Just hold the card within an inch or two of the contactless symbol on the terminal.

Using an ATM to get local currency (cash)

Be aware that credit cards usually charge interest from the moment you withdraw the money from an ATM, even if you pay the balance in full when due. Never use a credit card to get cash, unless you have absolutely no other option. Just like with a debit card, you'll need a 4-digit PIN code to use your credit card at an ATM machine. Be sure to get your PIN code from your credit card company prior to leaving the US.

Check with your bank about fees associated with your debit card. Your bank may charge you a fee when you use an out-of-network ATM. In addition, the ATM that you use may charge you a fee if you are outside of its network. Find out which ATMs (e.g. Cirrus, Maestro, Plus) are in your bank's network and look for in-network ATMs when traveling. It's easy to identify your ATM network. Look at the symbol on your debit card and match it to symbol on the ATM. Our Capital One 360 debit card has a Cirrus symbol.

To avoid foreign transaction and conversion fees, it's usually better to use a bank-affiliated ATM than others such as those that you might find in a market or on a street corner. Remember to look for ATMs with the same symbol as your debit card. If you end up at an ATM with high fees, you usually have the option to cancel the transaction before a final confirmation. Before you hit 'confirm', a notice of the amount of the fees will usually appear. If it feels too high, cancel and find a different ATM.

An important tip is to always keep enough cash on hand to buy a meal and pay for transportation for a day or two. We like to keep the equivalent of $100-$200 cash on hand in local currency, just in case we have a problem finding an ATM. We found that some cities and towns have more and/or easier access to bank ATMs, a lesson we learned while visiting Verona, Italy. We had most recently been in the similar-sized Tuscan town of Lucca where bank ATMs were plentiful and easy to find. To our surprise, we were unable to locate one in Verona. We wandered all over the historic section of the city and searched for an 'ATM near me' on the GPS. Luckily, we had enough cash on hand to make it through to our next destination.

Just as in the US, make sure you follow precautions to guard against anyone seeing your PIN number when you're getting cash at an ATM. Also, check to make sure the card entry slot is not 'fake.' Pull on it to make sure it is secured to the machine. If it comes off in your hand, you know it's a device to steal card information. Drop it and go to another ATM.

Disputing debit card charges?

In general, we use a credit card for purchases, such as, groceries, restaurant meals, museum entrance fees, and rail tickets. Another lesson learned... we used our debit card in a restaurant in Bolzano, Italy. The server took the card and swiped it through a point-of-purchase machine. He gave us back the card, but then said the transaction did not go through. This happened twice more. In the meantime, I checked my Capital One 360 app on my phone and saw that the charges were 'pending'. Language was an issue, and we were unable to resolve the multiple charges at that moment. Since the charges were listed as 'pending', I thought the bank might only charge us one time.

We went back to our hotel, and I called the bank. They said we needed to resolve the issue with the merchant because it was a debit charge, not a credit charge. We then went back to the restaurant the next day and spent an inordinate amount of time trying to convince the server that we had been overcharged. We had to insist on talking with the manager to finally get the multiple charges refunded. So...be very careful when using your debit card with merchants. It's not as simple to resolve erroneous charges as when you use a credit card.

Choosing a good credit card for European travel

Riomaggiore, Cinque Terre, Italy

When credit cards are accepted, almost all establishments in Europe take Visa or Mastercard. Your debit card is most likely a Visa or Mastercard. You can use it like a credit card, but remember that the money will immediately be withdrawn from your checking account. We have found that the best option is to have a credit card that:

- has no foreign transaction fees
- earns rewards points or cash back
- is a Visa or Mastercard
- is contactless

After our experience in Bolzano with the debit card, we obtained a Capital One Venture card. It's a Visa, and it's contactless. We earn points for purchases. The points can be redeemed for cash.

The rewards program is an important benefit to research when choosing your travel credit cards. We use the Platinum Delta American Express card whenever we can because we accrue Delta frequent flyer miles with each charge. The card has an annual fee ($250), but you receive a companion domestic flight ticket on Delta each year. We think this benefit more than pays for the annual fee. If you sign up for this card, be sure to do so when they are offering an incentive bonus, such as a large number of frequent flyer miles. Aside from the rewards, we enjoy American Express because we have always experienced amazing customer service with them.

Although both of our cards are free of foreign transaction fees, the American Express is not as widely accepted as the Visa in Europe. For example, we found that most places in Serbia and Croatia did not accept the American Express card.

Choosing your checking account bank

Because we travel most of the year now, we switched our checking account to a Capital One 360 account. We searched Google for best banks for Americans for international travel. Capital One was highly recommended, and we have been pleased, for the most part. With this debit card, we pay no foreign transaction or ATM fees for in-network ATMs when we're in

Europe (or in the US, for that matter).

Use a review service, such as NerdWallet, to learn about credit card options. NerdWallet currently recommends

Charles Schwab Bank as best for using ATMs
Capital One 360 as best for foreign transaction fees
HSBC Bank as best bank for ExPats
Citibank as best for wiring money

On the downside, we've had a few issues with our Capital One 360 account. First, it's primarily an online bank. There are some physical bank branches in some states, but they are rare. If you want to make a deposit, you do it by scanning the check with your phone. If you want to withdraw money, you use an ATM. Getting bills of specific denominations is not usually an option. We like to carry an emergency $100 bill and haven't figured out how to make an ATM give us a $100 bill...a small problem, but a limitation that we don't like.

A second major issue, if you're out of the country and attempt to access your account online (computer or mobile device), Capital One will send a verification code to your US mobile phone number. You must enter this verification code to access your account. I was locked out of viewing my account while we were traveling in Croatia, because I replaced my iPhone

Chateau de Chenonceau in the Loire Valley, France

SIM card with a Croatian SIM card. It was a smart decision because having a Croatian SIM card allowed me to use the GPS, make calls, receive texts, and access email for a very low Croatian rate. What I didn't realize was that I would not be able to receive anything through my US phone number (i.e. no verification codes from banks, credit cards, etc.) Obviously, if you remove the US SIM card, that number is no longer in the phone. We'll talk more about this in the communication chapter, but be aware that this is a limitation for Capital One and other vendors who use your cell phone number for verification. I called Capital One to see if they could send me email verifications instead, and they said no...only US mobile phone verifications.

Lastly, Capital One will not allow you to make deposits if you are out of the country. We found this out recently when we tried to deposit a AAA car insurance refund check while we were in England. The check had a 90-day expiration so we needed to deposit or cash it while we were traveling as we would not return home for 4 more months. Luckily, we learned that our Ameriprise brokerage account allows us to deposit checks. Problem solved, but it was another issue that made us unhappy with Capital One.

Summary tips for obtaining cash and using credit cards while traveling

- Use a bank-affiliated in-network ATM to obtain cash
- Use an ATM with the same symbol as your debit card whenever possible
- Do NOT choose the ATM currency conversion option
- Carry home some extra cash to use during your next visit
- Travel with a contactless Visa or Mastercard credit card that has no foreign transaction fees
- Use a credit card for as many purchases as you can to earn rewards and to manage disputed charges more easily
- Carry your checkbook with you to Europe and keep track of your debit charges and ATM withdrawals, just as you would at home

Buying through Amazon while in Europe

All you need to know is your local address, and you can buy from Amazon where ever you travel. Be sure to use the Amazon order site for that country. For example, if you're in the UK, go to www.Amazon.co.uk. You can use a search engine to find the correct Amazon site for the country in which you would like to receive a delivery. You may not have access to all of the exact same products that you buy in the US, but you should be able to find an acceptable substitute. You can certainly buy from Amazon using your US Amazon account, but you will avoid the high shipping fees if you use the local Amazon service. Just like in the US, read the description and the reviews for the products before you make purchases.

Here's a sample purchase process: Once you have selected your item(s) for purchase, proceed through the purchase process. If you're a Prime member, Amazon will ask you if you want a free trial membership in that country. I always say 'no', because there is usually an option for free shipping without Prime membership.

Remember to purchase the items in the local currency. Amazon will ask

FREE Click and Collect is available

Choose from 20 Amazon Pickup Locations near you.

Choose a delivery option:

Linda, we're giving you a 30-day free trial of Amazon Prime!

○ FREE Premium Delivery with Prime
  Fast, FREE Delivery prime : get it tomorrow, April 9

◉ FREE Standard Delivery : get it by Sunday, April 11

○ £4.99 Premium Delivery : get it tomorrow, April 9

Pay in USD

By placing your order you agree to Amazon's Conditions of Use & Sale. Please see our Privacy Notice, our Cookies Notice and our Interest-Based Ads Notice.

Order Summary

Items:	USD 32.89
Postage & Packing:	USD 6.17
Total:	USD 39.06
Promotion Applied:	-USD 6.17
Exchange rate guarantee fee:	USD 0.87

Order Total: **USD 33.76**
Order totals include VAT.See details.

Amazon Currency Converter

Enabled - Pay in USD
◉ USD 33.76 ○ GBP 23.90

Exchange rate
1 GBP = 1.4123560375 USD
(Includes the exchange rate guarantee fee)

☑ **By placing your order**, you agree to the Terms and Conditions of Amazon Currency Converter, provided by Amazon Services Europe, SARL. We will show you the option to pay in your card currency for eligible orders.

you if you want to buy in US dollars or in the local currency. The exchange rate will also usually be provided. In the below case, the purchase is small so the difference in conversion is relatively small. Using an online currency conversion calculator, you'll find that 23.90 pounds = 32.84 dollars at the current exchange rate. If I allow Amazon to convert for me, the price is $33.76, a little bit more.

Currency conversion is important to understand. It's quite possible that you will get less for your money if you allow merchants to do the conversion for you. Our credit card does not charge us foreign transaction fees, and we feel fairly confident that we are getting a better conversion rate through our American Express card. It's always smart to know the current exchange rate so that you can make an educated decision about accepting in-shop currency conversion. As a general practice, we never allow merchants to convert our charges to US dollars.

You can calculate the exchange rate for the local currency to US dollars with an online calculator. Here is an example.

https://www.xe.com/currencyconverter/

CHAPTER 9:
ESTIMATE YOUR
EUROPEAN TRIP BUDGET

Chapter 9: Estimate your European Trip Budget

- Overview of budget variables
  - Relative expensiveness of the destination
  - Air or cruise fare for travel to and from Europe
  - Transfer to and from airports or ship ports
  - First and second/standard class train travel
  - Private car and driver
  - Rental car
  - Accommodations/lodging
  - Guided tours and excursions – group or private
  - Motorcycle, bicycle, kayak, motorboat and other recreational vehicle rentals
  - Groceries, dining out, and snacks
  - Trip and health insurance
  - Management of the home in the US
  - Contingency fund for missed connections, last minute changes, minor injuries
- Strategies for allocating money for your trip
- Sample trip itinerary: 8 weeks in Italy with cost ranges

Two sets of travelers can plan the same travel itinerary, but have very different budgets. We have friends and family who like to travel first class all the way from airfare to staying at the Ritz Carlton to eating at Michelin-star restaurants to being chauffeured for private tours. That type of trip costs a lot more than one with less luxury. Interestingly, we've learned that greater luxury doesn't necessarily mean greater value or enjoyment. There's nothing wrong with being

The Cavern, Liverpool, England

140

pampered, but, if the budget is slimmer, think carefully about what's really important to your overall experience. One of the things that we keep in mind is that every dollar we spend on this trip is a dollar that we won't have to spend on a subsequent trip... and we plan on taking lots of trips.

Think about the experiences that you want to have, and then create a budget. We find this works better than simply setting aside a random amount of money and then rigidly planning not to overspend. Some

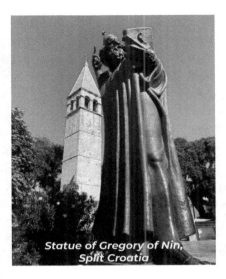

Statue of Gregory of Nin, Split Croatia

trips cost more than others, because of the things you want to do and the parts of the world you want to see. It would be a shame to travel all the way to a European city and decide not to see the main attraction because of cost. When you're deciding on your budget be sure to factor in tickets for items like a lift to the top of the Eiffel tower or a boat tour of Lake Geneva. Don't miss out on the big sites and events!

Here's an interesting way to view your travel budget...it really has more to do with your comfort level in spending and the style in which you want to travel than your money. If you have less funds to devote to travel, then spend time searching for discounts and consider traveling in the off season. If luxury is important, but you have a humble budget, consider traveling in some of the more affordable central or eastern European countries. Look for accommodations that are outside of the more expensive city centers. Choosing accommodations in nearby locations along train and bus lines can be an easy way to spend less, yet still have access to popular destinations.

Even if you have ample means, you might want to travel lightly and enjoy the frugality of hostels, monasteries, and camping sites. In Europe, you'll find plenty of retirees, not just students, enjoying these types of accommodations.

Of course, don't spend more than you can afford. You don't need to max out your budget to have a very enjoyable trip. You might be like us and be keen to get a "deal" whenever possible. To us a deal is when we receive really good value for our money...spending less than the value we believe we are receiving.

Take your time in creating your European trip. You may spend hours researching the best airfares and airport options. That's okay. Investing a lot of time in planning will help you save money and reduce unexpected issues in your travels. Let's start with an overview of some of the budget items discussed in other chapters. Again, think carefully about how you will travel and in what style.

Overview of budget variables

1. Relative expensiveness of the destination

Your money will go further in some countries than others. Here are some of the less and more expensive countries. In general, southern, central, and eastern Europe are less expensive than northern Europe.

Less expensive	More expensive
Bulgaria	Iceland
Romania	Switzerland
Poland	Norway
Montenegro	Denmark
Ukraine	Ireland
Portugal	Finland
Slovenia	Netherlands
Hungary	Sweden
Croatia	Italy
Czech Republic	United Kingdom
Serbia	France

2. Air or cruise fare for travel to and from Europe

The very first thing that you'll need to decide is where you want to go. If you don't have any preferences...you just want to go to Europe...then you might start by looking at the cost of flights from your nearest US airport to various European airports. Airfare is typically one of the bigger items in your travel budget, so, from that perspective, budget is an early consideration, both for destination and airfare.

You might also consider taking a transatlantic cruise, but that puts some real limits on your dates of travel and where you land. Cruises relocate from the states – usually Ft Lauderdale or Miami-- to Europe in April. Common ports in Europe are Barcelona and Civitavecchia (Rome). Ships "reposition" back to the States in late October or early November.

You can use booking engines to book your flights or cruises. Booking engines find prices and you can book through the booking engine (Expedia, Priceline, Hotwire). Aggregators—sites that do not book tickets, but instead search dozens of booking engines, airfare sites, and online travel agencies – are also good resources to consult. They compile the results. You identify the one you want and then click through to the booking site.

Here are some of the options you might consider in order of preference:

Skiplagged   --   aggregator
Momondo   --   aggregator and online travel agency
Skyscanner   --   aggregator
TripAdvisor   --   aggregator
Agoda   --   aggregator
Kayak   --   aggregator
Booking.com   --   aggregator
CheapOAir   --   online travel agency
Expedia   --   owns Travelocity and Orbitz – booking engine
Priceline   --   online travel agency and an aggregator

Search engines, such as the above, provide fares for a number of airlines and some even provide a calendar with variations in fare by day of month. Try using Google to search for flights and you'll have the options to see calendar dates with prices. You can adjust your trip to travel on the least expensive days if your schedule is flexible. If you have a preferred carrier, then look specifically for that carrier's lowest fares to Europe.

Also try broadening your search to nearby airports to compare fares. A number of major airports are relatively close to one another in Europe. For example, London Heathrow, London Gatwick, Paris Orly, and Paris Charles de Gaulle are not that far apart. The Eurostar train connects London and Paris. If you want to travel to that region, consider the cost of flying and adding a Eurostar train trip to transfer between cities.

Factors that affect airfare include

- time of year
- day of week that you want to travel
- number of connections
- cabin class
- baggage fees, taxes, etc..

Factors that affect cruise fares

- type of cabin, with inside cabins being the most economical
- meal plans
- add-ons – gratuities, alcohol, bottled water and sodas, internet connectivity
- transfers to and from airport
- airfare from home to the nearest airport to the port
- tours and excursions

Transatlantic repositioning cruise

You may have a preferred carrier and only want to fly on that carrier so that you earn frequent-flyer miles or enjoy other perks. For these reasons, we always use Delta. When I book flights, I start by looking at the hub or 'codeshare' partner hubs for Delta. For example, Air France-KLM and Virgin Atlantic are codeshare partners for Delta. Paris Charles de Gaulle is a hub for Air France-KLM.

Using the hubs in your airfare search can be important because you might be able to find direct flights from a US hub to a European hub for codeshare airlines. Flying between hubs is not necessarily less expensive, but it might mean less time in the air. Consider which is more important to you -- saving money or saving time. Personally, we like to look for shortest flight duration and lowest cost.

Oftentimes I call the Delta frequent flyer reservation assistance number to help me find the best rates after I've identified the specific region and a couple of different airports. For example, we like to travel to Lucca, Italy. It's a small medieval walled city in the Tuscany region. A few airports are options. Pisa is very nearby, but very small. A connector flight from a major European airport can take us to Pisa. It's possible to get direct flights from our home airport (Orlando) to Dublin, London, Paris, Frankfurt, Zurich, and a few others. We tend to fly to either London or Paris when traveling to Europe. Other options that usually require multiple flights could be Milan, Venice, Rome, or Florence. From any of those airports, we might take a connector flight to Pisa and/or a train to Lucca.

3. Transfer to and from airports or ship ports

When creating your budget, don't forget to include the cost of getting from the airport to your accommodations or ship port. Many airports in Europe have train stations attached, which makes it easy to book onward train travel to your accommodations. Most train stations have bus stops, which means you can get to smaller locales once you arrive at a nearby train station. Taxis are usually available at train stations as well.

Alternatively, you can ask your accommodation host if it's possible to book an airport or train station shuttle at an additional cost. We've always found this to be a good way to get from the airport to our lodging.

If you're taking a cruise, book the airport transfer when you book the cruise. It's worth the extra cost to have a cruise representative meet you at baggage claim, shepherd you to a bus, and then facilitate your check-in process for the cruise.

4. First and second/standard class train travel

It's usually not worth the extra money for a first-class train ticket, unless you are traveling for several hours. The 2nd class/standard seats are comfortable and adequate. In fact, many regional or inter-city trains only have 2nd class carriages. That said, we always buy a 1st class rail pass, because we like the option of traveling 1st class on long trips between major cities or from country to country. It costs about 20-25% more for a first class pass.

We usually buy a Eurail Pass, because of the convenience. It's not necessarily less expensive than buying tickets as you go, but it's very convenient to just hop on a train without stopping to buy tickets. It does happen that trains run late, which can then compress your connection time to the next train. Instead of waiting in long lines to buy a ticket, simply determine your departing train platform, and go directly to the train. There are a variety of passes with different costs that we discuss in the chapter on how to travel within Europe.

5. Private car and driver

On occasion, we've used a private car and driver to move us from city to city. Some countries have relatively inexpensive car services. We found drivers in Serbia and Croatia who were quite affordable. In contrast, a driver (Uber) in Wales, United Kingdom, was quite expensive. If it's your only option, then go with it, but try to find a train or bus that can get you where you want to go.

6. Rental car

If you're comfortable driving in Europe, then you may want to rent a car. Depending on where you're traveling, it could be comparable to buying regional flight, train, and bus tickets. However, keep in mind that you have to pay for parking, which can be steep. Also, some historic centers only allow cars with permits to drive in the center. You may have to park at a distance and walk in to some sites.

We haven't rented cars in Europe, but we have heard good reports from friends and relatives who have done so. It depends on your travel situation as to whether a rental car is a good option. If you have loads of luggage, lots of people in your party, remote destinations, then a rental car might be the best option. Read the fine print to make sure you understand all of the expenses involved in the rental (just like in the US). Many countries in Europe include liability insurance with the car rental; be sure to inquire about insurance when you rent. **Don't forget to get your international driver's license before you leave the States**.

Lastly, make sure that you have a reliable GPS for your rental car. Request an English-speaking GPS from the car rental agency. Inquire as to whether the GPS will work in remote areas and when you are traveling through tunnels. For example, friends reported being lost in a long tunnel in Switzerland when the GPS failed to signal their exit (yes, there are exits in tunnels in Switzerland). As a back-up, always write down the directions to your destination in case the GPS is not functioning well.

7. Accommodations/lodging

In our chapter on lodging, we discuss a number of strategies to find accommodations that meet your desired comfort level and budget. We usu-

Oxford Castle and Prison, Malmaison Hotel, Oxford, England

ally decide on a cost-per-night budget to help us identify the best options for us. Keep in mind that the amount per night will vary greatly by country. In more expensive countries, we often pay the equivalent of $200 per night, and, in less expensive countries, we aim for $75 per night. Larger cities cost more. Hotels are usually more expensive than apartments.

8. Guided tours and excursions – group or private

How much money do you want to spend on tours, museums, theatre, exhibits, cooking classes, and other tourist attractions? Sometimes it's most

Group cooking class with Chef Giuseppe, Extra Virgin, Lucca, Italy

cost efficient to book a guided tour through a company, like Viator, especially if you want to go places that are not accessible through public transportation. Use the internet to search for tours in the area. Visitor centers or visitor information offices are common in touristy areas, whether it's a large city or a small village. You can book tours through these offices or pick up maps and brochures. Your accommodation hosts or hotel concierge are also good resources for finding good guides and tours.

If you're taking a cruise, plan to go on a number of excursions. It would be a shame to travel all the way to spectacular European destinations and not learn about the culture and history. Cruises usually offer excellent excursion options that allow you to optimize your time while in port. In addition, you can eliminate the worry of being left behind if something happens and you get delayed while you're seeing the sites. For example, our excursion bus was unable to move forward in Palermo, Sicily, because of a large protest. Our entire group on the bus had to disembark and walk back to the ship. It caused a delay in leaving the port, but no one was left behind.

9. Motorcycle, bicycle, kayak, motorboat and other recreational vehicle rentals

Consider renting a Vespa, kayak, or other recreational vehicle to enjoy national parks, alpine lakes, or seaside resorts. Use Google or another search engine to help you estimate how much to add to your budget for these types of tours or rentals. You may be able to find very affordable guided bicycle or motorcycle tours. We've been on several sea kayaking tours. It's a great way to enjoy a new area.

10. Groceries, dining out, and snacks

We usually find that we spend much less on food in Europe than in the US, whether dining out or buying groceries. Junk food is more or less the same price, but locally grown, organic, fresh high quality food is usually way cheaper in Europe. You could estimate your food budget at about 2/3 of what you normally spend in the US during a comparable period of time.

11. Trip and health insurance

Brian bicycling on the walls of Lucca, Italy

See the chapter on insurance for more information. We're including it in our list so that you don't forget to budget for trip and health insurance.

12. Management of the home in the US (community watch, house sitter, pet sitter, yard care)

You'll no doubt have some extra expenses to consider when leaving your home for a period of time. Build these expenses into your trip budget. Will you need to kennel your pet? Does your community watch service charge a fee? Will you pay a house sitter or neighborhood friends to help you water plants or watch your house? Think about any extra costs that you might incur at home and add them to the budget.

13. Contingency fund for missed connections, last minute changes, minor injuries

We usually plan for about a 10% contingency to absorb unexpected problems that arise or to take advantage of unexpected opportunities.

Strategies for allocating money for your trip

Perhaps you have a broad budget item for travel in your annual spending plan already. That's a great place to start, but you might have even more money to spend on traveling if you add up the things that you will NOT be buying at home when on the road. For each week that you travel, consider what you would have spent on groceries, dining out, gasoline, entertainment, clothing, etc. and add that amount to what you can spend on your trip. If you normally spend $200 per week on groceries and dining out, then add $200 for each week of your trip. Do the same for any other non-fixed expenses that you will not incur while traveling. With this strategy, you can significantly increase the budget for your trip without hurting your annual spending plan.

Sample trip itinerary: 8 weeks in Italy with costs

The following is an itinerary from a prior trip. It demonstrates the type of information that we include in our travel document. We build it as we go; each time we book a reservation, we add to the document. In the end, our finished product keeps us on track each day with all the relevant information for getting to places, finding our accommodations, and remembering what has been paid in advance and what has not. In addition, the itinerary not only serves as a plan and guide for us, it also serves as information for family and friends-- minus the budgetary aspects of the itinerary. We email an abbreviated itinerary so they are generally aware of our whereabout for emergency purposes.

8 Weeks in Italy Itinerary and Budget (excluding food and tours)

	Two month Eurail Global Pass1st class	$2114
	World Nomad Travel Insurance	$638.45
	Car to airport	$85 each way
	Depart Orlando to Gatwick Virgin Air Flt VS16 Two passengers	Premium Economy Fare total: $3564.26
Day 1	Arrive Gatwick at 9:05 am in the North Terminal. Clear customs. Take the inter-terminal shuttle to South Terminal and then the train station is nearby.	
Day 2	CitizenM London Shoreditch, 6 Holywell Lane, London England EC2A 3ET	Pd $138.12
Day 3	Take a taxi to the St Pancras train station.	20 pounds
	Take the Eurostar to Paris (3 hrs 23 mins) Train 9018	train reservations $96.76 for two

Day 3	ibis Beauvais Aeroport 1 rue Jacques Goddet, Beauvais Oise 60000	$53.89
Day 4	Ryanair from Beauvais to Pisa for two passengers	266.55 Euros /$294.59
Day 4	Take the Pisa People Mover to train station. Buy ticket at kiosk on shuttle track.	2.70 euro each
	Take the 3:20 train that will arrive at 3:47 in Lucca.	Use rail pass
28 nights	Il Loft di Andrea (ground floor apartment) Via San Georgio	2 adults, 28 nights $2049.73 Ins $59.00 Ins $91.96 For transaction fee $61.49 Pay tax to host upon check in
Day 33	Take the train from Lucca to Riomaggiore, Cinque Terre	Write the trip in each Eurail pass book before boarding the train
Day 33-34	Alla Marina s.n.c. di Sandro Pasini e Andrea Pasini website: www.allamarina.com e-mail: info@allamarina.com Room5 for 2 nights	Total cost euro 300 ($365.44) by cash at check in.
Day 35	train from Riomaggiore to Sestri Levante at 8:24 – 9:19 Sestri Levante to Roma Termini 9:38 to 14:33 Roma Termini to Naples 14:48 to 15:58 Subway to Sorrento Walk to hotel	Write the trip in each Eurail pass book before boarding the train
Day 35	Ulisse Deluxe Hostel Via del Mare, 22, Sorrento, NA, 80067 Italy	$133.18

Day 36	Ferry to Capri (45 minutes). Get a bus ticket on the island and take a bus up to Anacapri	40 euros for two people 2 euros each for bus
Day 36-38	Anacapri-- Il Tramonto (The Sunset) B & B, Via Migliera, 30/B80071 Anacapri (NA) Italy Tel. 333 1742184/334 7125862 Superior Double Room, Jetted Tub, Continental Breakfast Free Wireless Internet, 1 Double Bed NONSMOKING_ROOM	$425.43 3 nights
Day 39	Take the bus down to Capri port Take the ferry to Naples (50 minutes) 10:10- 11:00 am Take the train from Naples to Paestum – 12:46-14:02 (no reservation needed)	2 euros each 20 euros each Use rail pass
Day 39	Paestum (oldest temples in Europe – 500 BC) Il GranaiodeiCasabella Via Tavernelle 84, Capaccio-Paestum, SA, 84063 Italy Superior Double Room Breakfast Buffet Free Wireless Internet Free Parking 1 Double Bed NONSMOKING_ROOM	$100.58
Day 40	Take the train from Paestum to Battipaglia 8:50-9:09 am Battipaglia to Taranto 9:38-12:55 (1st class coach 2 seats 55,56) Taranto to Brindisi 14:02-15:06 Brindisi to Lecce 15:58-16:28 Taxi to hotel	Write the trip in each Eurail pass book before boarding the train 10 euros for taxi
Day 41	Full-Day Cisternino, Alberobello&Polignano a Mare Tour through GetYourGuide Duration 8 hours 2 AdultsThey will pick us up at our hotel. Includes lunch. Does not include gratuities.	US$ 434.34

Day 43	taxi to the train station	10 euros taxi
	Take the 6:06 am train from Lecce to arrive in Bologna Centrale at 13:15 on Trenitalia	Train reservation $28.08 Write the trip in each Eurail pass book before boarding the train
	No reservation needed for Bologna Centrale 14:10 pm – Bolzano 17:30 pm	
Day 43-45	Bolzano Residence Fink, Mustergasse 9, Bolzano, 39100 Italy	$283.20 3 nights
Day 46	Train from Bolzano to Verona (approximately 1 ½ hours)	Write the trip in each Eurail pass book before boarding the train
Day 46-47	Verona MyPlace Duomo Apartments Sep 27, 2019- Sep 29, 2019 , 1 room | 2 nights Via Duomo, 4, Verona, VR, 37121 Italy	2 nights$270.89
Day 47	Train from Verona to Milan (approx. 1 hr 15 min	Write the trip in each Eurail pass book before boarding the train
Day 47-48	Milan/CuggionoResidenzaSant'Anna Via San Rocco 71/75/20012 Cuggiono 1 bedroom apartment with balcony	2 nights US $183.53 VAT $18.35 Total $201.88
	Email info@residenzasantanna.it to make arrangements for shuttle pick up at the train station	
Day 49	Train from Milan to Turin (approx. 1 hour)	Write the trip in each Eurail pass book before boarding the train
Day 49-51	Turin Residence Sacchi Basic Studio, Full Kitchen, 1 Double Bed, Non-Smoking	3 nights $284.40

Day 52	Train from Turino Porto Susa to Paris Gare Lyon 10:11 to 16:11 on the high speed train – 0 changes Extra reservation charge	Write the trip in each Eurail pass book before boarding the train $107.16
Day 52-54	OKKO Hotels Paris Gare de l'Est, Paris 30 A rue d'Alsace, Paris 75010	$402.08 3 nights
Day 55	Take Eurostar from Paris Gare du Nord 10:13 am to 11:43 am London St Pancras Take the Victoria tube line to Vauxhall station Take the train to Windsor/Eton Riverside	96.76 for two Use Oyster card Write the trip in each Eurail pass book before boarding the train
Day 55-56	The Crown and Cushion 84 Hight Street, Windsor, England, SL4 6AF United Kingdom Compact Double Room Ensuite (Room 7) Includes: Full Breakfast Free Wireless Internet Free Parking	$175.14 2 nights
Day 57	Train from Windsor to Gatwick 8:21 am Windsor Riverside to Clapham Junction 9:08 am (no reservation needed) 9:23 am Express to Gatwick Airport 9:47 am (reservations are optional on this train) Arrive in the South Terminal and take the shuttle to the North terminal	Write the trip in each Eurail pass book before boarding the train
Day 58	Gatwick to Orlando Zone A North Terminal Flight number VS15 Depart Gatwick at 1 pm and arrive in Orlando at 5:20 pm Driver will check the plane landing time and pick us up at baggage claim on the 2nd floor.	$85

CHAPTER 10:
BEFORE YOU GO: TIPS FOR TRAVEL PREPARATION

Chapter 10: Before you go: Tips for travel preparation

- Take care of your US home
- Plan important communication before you go
  - Know the local emergency phone numbers
  - Plan for cell phone and internet access
- Plan the sights you want to see
- Plan use of public transportation in advance
- Packing
  - Take the right technology and equipment
  - Pack a minimal amount of clothing and do laundry regularly
  - Organize all of your travel plans and documents

Take care of your US home

If you have other people or family members living in your US home, you probably won't need to worry about maintenance of your home, bringing in the mail, home security, etc. For those of us who will potentially leave an empty house, here are some tips and suggestions:

- Home insurance: Check with your homeowner's insurance to identify restrictions on your coverage if the house is vacant for a period of time. Our homeowner's insurance agent told us that the policy assumes we occupy the house 365 days a year. If anything goes awry, the insurance company can avoid paying any claims if the house is unoccupied for 30 days or more.

- House sitters: Enlist the aid of a house sitter. We have a friend who stays in our house while we're away. Interestingly, our home owner's insurance views a house sitter like they would a renter. This interpretation resulted in an increase in our premium. Our policy will still cover any mishaps or damage, but the premium is higher because the house is not owner occupied 365 days a year.

- House sitter agreement: We don't pay our house sitter so he is not an employee. He doesn't pay rent, so he's not a tenant. Be sure to use a house-sitting agreement that outlines the specifics of your agreement with the house sitter and your expectations for their stay.

- Mail: Our house sitter checks our mail and alerts us to anything that looks important. We ask him to open it, send us a picture of the item, and then help us as needed with anything that requires attention. Alternatively, you could forward your mail to a friend or relative. You could also just place a hold on the mail and take care of it when you return home.

- Alternate mail monitoring: Rent a mailbox from an online company. This is a great strategy if you will be gone for a long period of time. There are many companies from which to choose. Here's how it works:
  - Forward your mail to their address.
  - Do Changes of Address for all of your mail.
  - The mail service company will receive your mail and notify you it has arrived.
  - You have the choice of having it scanned (for a fee), having it forwarded (for a fee) or discarding it.

- Renting home: Renting out your home while you're away may impact your insurance and property taxes. In Florida, if we rented out our home, we would lose our homestead exemption for property taxes, we would owe sales tax on the rent, and our insurance premium would be higher. In addition, a property management company would need to be paid a percentage of the rent. With those expenses, renting would likely not be profitable, and we would have the additional worry of having strangers living in our home. Consider all of these factors before deciding to rent out your home.

- Community Watch: Some communities have an organized security service or set of neighbors. Alert them and pay any associated fees for the service of having your home checked on a regular basis.

Plan important communication before you go

Many countries in Europe teach English as a school subject, so locals have some fluency. You can usually get by using English in restaurants, grocery stores, train stations, and tourist attraction ticket offices. However, don't count on it. Try to learn some very important phrases ...where is the toilet? May we have the check please? How much does this cost? Please. Thank you. Hello. Goodbye.

In smaller cities and villages, you will likely encounter locals who do not speak English. Be prepared to communicate what you need by writing down frequent and common questions on notecards. Use Google translate to write the question(s) in the local language. Some questions are likely to be used over and over (Where is the toilet? Which direction is the train station?). Even though you don't speak the language, the locals will appreciate that you took the time to plan to communicate in their language. Unfortunately, Americans sometimes are stereotyped as being a little insensitive about other cultures and languages. Prove them wrong by making the effort to try.

Where is the toilet?	Dov'e la toilette?
How much does this cost?	Quanto costa questo?
Thank you very much	Grazie Mille

If you have cellular service while you're out and about, you may be able to ask Siri (your smart phone) to say what you need. We've used this strategy before. You can ask your phone to translate from English to the local language. The responder can then ask it to translate from the local language to English when they answer. As I'm writing this chapter, it's 2021 and my guess is that options for communication will continue to evolve rapidly.

Know the local emergency phone numbers

Before you travel, create a cheat sheet with emergency numbers and information for all of the countries that you will be visiting. Print it out and keep it with you in your purse or messenger bag. You can also keep a copy on your phone as a Word doc or in the 'files' folder. The important point is hat you need to have a copy handy in an emergency; that's why I like to eep a paper copy in my purse. Here is an example:

'oland Numbers to call in an emergency

.12 is the European emergency phone number, available everywhere in he EU, free of charge. You can call 112 from fixed and mobile phones to :ontact any emergency service: an ambulance, the fire brigade or the po-ice. In Poland 112 calls are answered by the Fire Brigade and Police.

\longside 112, the following emergency numbers are available:

- 999 – ambulance
- 998 – fire brigade
- 997 – police

:mergency Line (for foreigners only in the summer season): +48 608 599)99, +48 800 200 300
Tourist Helpline – provides tourist information as well as aid in emergen-:ies, e.g. connected to lost documents, finding urgent medical treatment, -oad assistance, etc. +48 222 787 777, +48 608 599 999
n case of emergency, you may also contact U.S. Consulate in Poland:
J.S. Consulate General in Krakow address:
Jlica Stolarska 9; Krakow, Poland
Contact:
Telephone: (48) (12) 424-5100
Fax: (48) (12) 424-5103
After-hours emergencies: (48) 601-483-348

The Balkan languages are very similar so you can use many of the same phrases in Bosnia-Herzegovina, Serbia, and Croatia. These countries com-prised the former Yugoslavia.

Bosnia and Herzegovina Medical and Emergency Information
Police: Dial 122
Fire: dial 123.
Ambulance: Dial 124 or 611-1111
In the event of a serious medical emergency, take the following steps:
1. Call 124 or 611-111.

2. State "I have an emergency and need an ambulance" (Ja trebam hitnu pomoć).

Speak slowly and clearly when speaking with the operator. Stay calm and describe the situation.

For example:

"My friend, spouse, child is having ... "

Chest Pain (Bol u grudima)

Trouble Breathing (Problem sa disanjem)

Unconscious (Bez svijesti)

Bleeding (Krvarenje)

Serious Injury (Ozbiljna povreda)

Head, neck, back (Glava, vrat, leđa)

Possible Poisoning (Moguće trovanje)

3. State your specific address: My address is ... Moja adresa je ...

4. Give the name of the patient.

When an ambulance is called, the call routes through the Institute of Emergency Medical Care in Sarajevo, which will decide whether the patient should come to the Institute or go to the nearest hospital. The doctor is also available to give medical advice over the phone. The number of calls, traffic conditions, and the weather may affect ambulance response time. Calls will be triaged according to severity; so please be as clear as possible on the patient's condition.

Medical Emergency Phrases

English (Bosnian)

Emergency (Hitno)

I don't speak Bosnian (Ne govorim Bosanski)

Do you speak English (Da li govorite Engleski)

I need an ambulance (Ja trebam hitnu pomoć)

My address is (Moja adresa je)

Please get a doctor quickly (Molim vas dovedite doktora brzo)

Please take me to the hospital (Molim vas odvedite me u bolnicu)

I have (Ja imam)

Serious injury (Ozbiljna povreda)

head, neck, back (glava, vrat, leđa)

Possible poisoning (Moguće trovanje)

Chest Pain (Bol u grudima)

Trouble Breathing (Problem sa disanjem)
Unconscious (Bez svijesti)
Bleeding (Krvarenje)
Heart attack (Infarkt srca)

American Citizen Services
U.S. Embassy Sarajevo
1 Robert C. Frasure Street
71000 Sarajevo
Tel: +387 33 704 000
E-mail: sarajevoacs@state.gov

Serbia
Belgrade
Police department: dial 192
Fire department: dial 193
Ambulance department: dial 194
It should be kept in mind that if you dial from a mobile phone, you might need to add the Belgrade calling code prefix 011. For example, if you need to call the police you will dial 011192.
Besides these, you can also dial the European emergency number 112. As of recently, this number exists in Serbia, and because it was a project of EU, operators also speak English. They are specially trained to work there, and they will take your case, and transfer it to the department that is needed. In case you do not know where you are, they will determine your location.

Croatia
112 is one of the emergency numbers in Croatia.
The national emergency numbers are:
192- police.
193- fire brigade,
194- ambulance,
195- search and rescue at sea,
1987- road assistance.
US Embassy in Croatia In Case of Emergency
The Consular Section is open from 8:00-4:30. If you need immediate assistance for a life or death emergency involving an U.S. citizen, please call

+385 1 661 2345 between the hours of 8:00 am and 4:30 pm. To reach a duty officer outside of working hours dial +385-1-661-2200.

Italy

To report the injury, illness, death or arrest of a U.S. Citizen, or to request emergency assistance for a U.S. citizen, please contact the Duty Officer at: Embassy ROME & Consulate General FLORENCE – If you are an American citizen with an after-hours emergency in Rome or Florence, or calling about someone who is in these consular district, please call the switchboard in Rome at 06-46741 (from within Italy) or 011-39-06-46741 (from the U.S.). Consulate General MILAN – If you are an American citizen with an after-hours emergency or calling about someone who is in Milan's consular district, please call the switchboard at 02-290351 (from within Italy) or 011-39-02-290351 (from the U.S.).

Consulate General NAPLES – If you are an American citizen with an after-hours emergency and are within the Naples' consular district or calling about someone who is in the Naples consular district, please call the switchboard at 081-583-8111 (from within Italy) or 011-39-081-583-8111 (from the U.S.).

Just in case you have an emergency in Italy, here are the numbers to call and some of the phrases you might need to say.

You can report anything on 112, the single European emergency number, whose operators will direct you to the relevant services.

But knowing the direct number to call could get you a faster response in a situation where time is critical.

Here are the main phone numbers you'll need to report an emergency in Italy.

What is Italy's equivalent of 999 or 911? Within Italy, the general number for all emergencies – the equivalent of 999 in the UK or 911 in the US – is 113.

This nationwide number connects you to the state police (Polizia di Stato), the civil police force that will assist you not only if you're reporting a crime but for any other kind of emergency too.

• Plan for cell phone and internet access

After numerous trips to Europe, we've had a few realizations about using cellular service in Europe. First, it's usually expensive to use our US carrier cellular service. We learned last fall that turning on roaming to locate restaurants or hotels nearby, using the GPS when we got lost, sending the occasional text, checking emails occasionally when not on WiFi, and other common uses of our phones, resulted in two large mobile phone bills (approximately $300 each month). The very best way to get affordable service is to find places where you can connect to free WiFi. Some cities in Europe have free WiFi in the city centers. Check with the local tourist information office.

More important than the cost of using cellular was that, even when we turned on international roaming for cellular service, we seldom got a signal. That might be because Europe uses a different cellular network. It might also depend upon which country one is visiting. It didn't work well for us in Serbia or Croatia. Depending on your US cellular service carrier, you may need to let them know which countries you'll be traveling in prior to leaving the US.

It occurred to us that having phone service could be an important safety issue. What if we're separated while traveling and need to call or text each other? What if one of us gets hurt while we're out hiking and no one else is around? What if we can't find a free WiFi hotspot when we need to find our apartment host to let them know we need to check in?

For all of these reasons, we decided to get local SIM cards for our phones while we were in Croatia. A T-mobile retail space was nearby to our accommodations, and we were able to get a pre-paid plan on a SIM card. Surprisingly, prepaid SIM cards were very inexpensive in Croatia. We opted for the maximum GB plan for 30 days...1000GB. There was a cost for the SIM card and then the cost for the data. The total for our 2 phones was $37.50 for the first month. The next month's data fee was a few dollars less because we had already paid for the SIM cards.

A downside was that our iPhone XRs only had one physical SIM card port. We had to remove (and save in a safe place) our US SIM cards, which meant that we were no longer able to send/receive texts or phone calls with our US phone numbers. To make sure that we received communications from family and friends, we sent an email letting them know that our US phone lines were not in service. If they wanted to contact us, they could use email, Facebook Messenger, Zoom, or our Croatian number with WhatsApp or Viber.

We have since learned how to use the second SIM port in an iPhone; it's an electronic port. You may have to contract for a longer phone service if you use the electronic SIM port. As of summer 2021, the best strategies to connect to the Internet and/or make phone calls is to

1) use the WiFi in your accommodations,
2) find a nearby free WiFi café or restaurant, or
3) buy a cheap phone in the country in which you're spending the most time and then buy a pre-paid SIM card.

Plan the sights you want to see

We often start with a rough draft of our itinerary for each stop before we even leave the States. Use the internet to help you decide which sites you need to see in a city or region. A good app is "Visit a City." It provides the top sites, brief descriptions, an itinerary with recommended timing, and directions from site to site. We often consult the app prior to leaving the states and then print out itineraries for cities or regions that have lots of different things we want to see.

TripAdvisor is another good app. You can research sites that you want to see and read reviews from other travelers. Rick Steve's has a similar forum on his travel site.

Plan your use of public transportation in advance of leaving your lodging

Don't count on having cellular service as you're roaming around a city or the countryside. We frequently find that our connection to the internet is great with WiFi, but unreliable with our cellular service. That means, our GPS is usually not available when we're wandering around.

We have a few strategies for navigating. First, plot your routes in advance of leaving your lodging when you're connected to the Internet and use GPS hrough WiFi. If you're already away from your lodging, find a restaurant or café with free WiFi. Use the Maps app or Google Maps on your phone.

Click on the details icon so that the turn-by-turn directions are listed. Now, take screen shots to capture the entire route as a set of photos. You can "photo" the listed directions as well as the map directions. When you create photos of the map, make sure that you zoom in enough to capture the names of the streets. As you wander around, you can easily access your photos to see the directions. You don't need an internet connection to access your photos.

The computer is plugged into a voltage converter

Packing

• Take the right technology and equipment

  • Electricity voltage converters and plug adapters. The power system in Europe uses a different voltage than in the United States. American appliances run on 110 volts, European on 220, and United Kingdom on 230 or higher. Read the label on your hair dryer, shaver, computer, etc. to see if it has a power voltage range, such as 110-220. You may be able to use your item in both the US and Europe, but don't count on it. We pack a power converter for different voltage in addition to power adapters for different plugs.

  • Portable chargers and power banks. Take along a couple of chargers and power banks for your phones, tablets, e-readers, etc. Be sure to buy one that is trustworthy – read the reviews, don't buy a cheap one, make sure it's compatible with your phones and other technology. We have a charger for our iPhones that is made specifically for our new iPhone 12s.

  • Apple product plugs. According to Apple, you don't need a voltage converter for Apple products, just the socket adapters. Be sure to check on your specific Apple products before using the power voltage while you're traveling. Apple says "Apple USB power adapters are designed for use with power sources rated to provide 100V AC to 240V AC at 50Hz to 60Hz. The Type A (flat parallel-blade design) Apple 5W USB, 18W, and 20W USB-C power adapters, as well as the 10W and 12W USB power adapters (with Type A AC plug attached) also comply with the IEC/UL 60950-1 and IEC/UL 62368-1 standards for use with power sources rated to provide 115V AC at 400Hz."

- Smart phones, tablets, and electronic readers. Minimize the amount of extra written material in your luggage by saving electronic copies to your smart devices. It's okay to carry along a hard copy of your reservations, maps, tour tickets, etc., but work towards relying on electronic copies to save room and weight in your luggage. It's also easier to find all of your documents if they are on your phone or tablet. Also, books definitely add weight so electronic readers are the optimal way to carry along multiple books, including guidebooks and cultural information to learn about the area you're visiting.

- Electronic shavers and hair dryers. Be sure to plug your shaver and hair dryer into your power converter, unless the appliance specifically says that it's plug is compatible with the local voltage.

- Pack a minimal amount of clothing and do laundry regularly

Before packing, make a list of the types of activities you'll be doing while traveling. Here is an example list of activities that we use as we prepare to pack:
- Exercise walking and bike riding
- Walking and sight-seeing (museums, churches, historic centers, etc.)
- Traveling on the airplane, train, and bus
- Lounging/reading/working on our blog at 'home'
- Dining at casual and moderately dressy restaurants

Once you have a list of your activities, you can list the type of clothes you'll need.

Exercise walking and bike riding	Exercise shorts (1) Exercise leggings (1) T-shirts (2) Sports bra (1) Walking sneakers or shoes Athletic socks (2)
Walking and sight-seeing (museums, churches, historic centers, etc.)	Skirts (2) Jeans/pants (2) Sleeveless Tops (2) ¾ or long sleeve tops (2) Pashmina to cover shoulders Walking sandals or ankle boots
Traveling on the airplane, train, and bus	Compression socks Cardigan sweater
Lounging/reading/working on our blog at 'home'	Pajama top and long pants Leggings L/S t-shirt
Dining at casual and moderately dressy restaurants	Casual dress or skirt & top with pashmina or cardigan
Miscellaneous items	Lightweight rain coat Pashmina Underwear and t-shirts or bras Denim jacket Roll-up puff jacket in a pouch

When booking travel, try to find places that include laundry facilities. If the apartment or hotel doesn't have laundry facilities, then use the Internet to find a nearby laundry service. Stop by to see if they will wash and fold your clothes for you so that you don't lose a day of your sight-seeing doing laundry.

Other packing items

Technology	Smart phone
	Tablet and/or e-reader
	Computer, if you're working or blogging
	Ear buds
	Relevant cords
	Voltage converter
	Plug adaptors
	Portable power charging bank for smart phones, etc.
Toiletries	Washcloth
	Make-up wipes
	Travel size toothpaste, mouth wash, tooth brush, dental floss
	Travel size deodorant, shampoo, conditioner, shaving cream, soap
	Razor
	Make-up (think about what you'll really use each day and minimize what you pack)
Medicines	Ample supply of prescription meds
	Over-the-counter pain reliever (e.g. Advil), Imodium, Pepto Bismol
	(note: you can buy OTC meds in any pharmacy in Europe...no need to pack)
	Any nutritional supplements that you take on a regular basis
Miscellaneous	Large coffee mug that can also be used for soup or oatmeal
	Spoon, fork, dinner knife
	Instant coffee sleeves, instant creamer, sweetener (if needed)
	Snacks (nuts, protein bars...no agricultural produce)
	Reusable washable bags for groceries and toting other things
	Compact umbrella
	Sun and/or rain hat
	Gloves for cold weather

- Organize all of your travel plans and documents

First, create an itinerary that includes all of your day-to-day travel plans. Use a Word doc or an Excel spreadsheet. Save your itinerary as an electronic document on your phone and your tablet in the files app. Also, consider saving a copy to a cloud service, such as Google drive. If you save it to Google drive, you can share access to the document with friends and family. Print a copy and carry it in your purse (or man-bag). Place another copy in your luggage.

Next, be sure that you save all of your reservation confirmation emails to a folder in your email box. I have a folder named 'travel'. Brian creates folders for each trip. The important thing is that you save the emails in a place where you can easily access the information when checking in or making changes to reservations.

If you bring a hard copy of all of your reservations, consider getting a lightweight folder with a clasp. I use a folder to carry printed documents, money from countries we'll be visiting, copies of our passports, and any other essential documents. The folder is packed with my laptop in my carry-on bag and keeps things nicely organized.

CHAPTER 11:
TRAVEL PLANNING TIMELINE AND CHECKLIST

Chapter 11: Travel planning timeline and checklist

4 to 6 months prior to departure	Read Chapter: What do you want to do and where do you want to go? • Embrace the retirement travel mindset • Identify your travel preferences • Describe how you like to spend your time • Identify the best region of Europe to do your favorite things • Decide how much time you will spend on the trip and when you will travel • Complete the checklist for the ideal travel experience • Review our general guidelines for travel

	Read Chapter: Planning your European trip
	• Options: Ponder planned itineraries vs free-form travel
	  • Let someone else plan your trip?
	  • Plan Your Own Trip: Nomadic roaming or day trips from a home-base
	• Choose your European travel destination for your next trip
	• Just do it! Plan your next trip to Europe
	Research airfare or cruise fares
	Book your cruise (consider the cruise/fly package for potential savings on airfare) and consider adding the transfer excursion to get you from the airport to the ship
	Book flight reservations

	If not taking a cruise, decide between planned itineraries vs free-form travel Book your guided travel tour Or Begin booking accommodations for your free-form trip if you're traveling to a highly desirable place in high season
2-months out	Book accommodations if you have not done so already
	Develop plan for managing your US household while traveling • Find a house sitter and create a house sitter agreement

	• Make arrangements for short-term rental to friends, family, visiting professors • Consult your homeowner's insurance for rules for vacant properties or non-home owner occupied properties
	Set up auto-pay for household bills, if not already done
	Research day trips, activities, tours, excursions that might need to be pre-booked and book as desired (Note: On cruises, excursions usually cost extra and must be booked in addition to the cruise. Highly desirable excursions frequently sell out so book early.)
1-month out	Book accommodations, if not yet done
	Continue exploring day trips, activities, tours, excursions that might need to be pre-booked and book as desired.
	Identify travel wardrobe and purchase any desired items
	Purchase relevant power plug adaptors and voltage converters (Note: You may want to purchase your converter in Europe. Be sure that your converter has a European plug. If going to the UK, get a converter with a UK plug.)
	Ask your physician for enough prescription medications to cover your absence from home
	Ask your physician about any recommended over-the-counter meds to take with you in case of minor illnesses (e.g. Imodium, Pepto Bismol, Advil, Tylenol, Pepcid) Make sure your booster shots are up to date
	Place a hold on your mail, if no one is picking up your mail for you, or have it forwarded to a trusted person who will manage your mail while you're away
1-week out	Notify community watch and/or neighbors if you do not have a house sitter

Evaluate the security of your US home. Consider purchasing timers for lights around the house and set them to go on and off throughout the night. Consider motion detector lights for the exterior and garden areas.

Alert your bank and credit cards that you are traveling internationally
Tell your cell phone carrier which countries you'll be traveling in

Make sure your checking account has sufficient funds to cover any budgeted ATM withdrawals and automated payments that will occur during your trip

Pack your travel wardrobe. Decide if you have too much luggage to comfortably carry. Eliminate anything that is not absolutely essential.

Buy knee-high compression socks that are meant for travel to wear on the plane to avoid blood clots

Leave room in your luggage for all toiletries, medications, power adaptors/converters, and your technology (e.g. power cords, laptop, e-reader, iPad, iPod, air buds). Consider taking a carry on with all of these items (except liquids).

Book a car to the airport or arrange for airport parking

Arrange for transport from airport or cruise port to your accommodation in Europe

Make 2 sets of photocopies of your passports, credit card numbers and contact information, and driver license. Give a copy to your trusted relative or friend in the US along with your itinerary. Pack the other copy securely in your carry-on bag.

Make a list of all the last-minute things that you need to pack

1-day out

Review your list of last-minute things to pack. Have you packed everything you need?

Unpack and then repack your suitcase ... Again, eliminate anything that is not absolutely necessary. Keep in mind that you might want to purchase clothes on your trip. Also, you can wash your clothes to wear them multiple times while traveling. Make sure your luggage is not too heavy for you to carry.

Gather all of your power cords, adaptors, toiletries, medications, supplements, etc. and pack in your carry-on bag. Make sure they are easy to access for removal during your airport security screening.

Purchase and pack any food items that you want to take with you. Find the rules on the government website for your entry country to learn which foods are allowed (e.g. meat and fruits are not allowed in the UK). Most countries allow nuts and protein bars.

Pack extra items that are not essential, but that you might greatly miss on longer travels (e.g. favorite coffee mug, lifestraw cup for filtered water, snacks to eat on plane, instant coffee sleeves, instant creamer, sweetener)

Check weather and evaluate the outerwear needs for your travel destination (e.g. raincoat, rainhat, umbrella, gloves, scarves, windbreakers) and pack in your carry-on bag or wear on the plane.

Make note of the contact and reservation information for your transport from the airport to your accommodations and place the note in an easily accessible place (e.g. the notes app on your phone or written on a piece of paper in your carry-on luggage).

Reconfirm your ride to your local airport and your pickup at your destination airport, if applicable.

Create and print out a document with your name, mobile telephone number, email address, and the name & address of your initial accommodation in Europe. Use large type to make the information stand out if your baggage is somehow lost and someone finds it. Place this sheet on top of your belongings before you close the suitcase. Make one copy per bag.

If you think your driver at your destination may not speak English, use Google translate to create and print a notecard with a request to take you to your accommodation in the relevant language. Keep this in a handy place, such as your purse or pocket.

Do an Internet search for your arrival airport and explore the layout. Look for your path from your arrival terminal >>> baggage claim >>> passport control >>> customs >>> the arrival hall.
Research how you will reach the car service driver, the car rental counter, the bus, or train station. Does an airport shuttle take you to a main terminal? Where is the pick-up location for ground transportation? How do you get to the car rental counter? Write down the instructions in detail for how you walk from your airplane to your mode of transportation that will take you to your accommodation.

Make sure your directions for getting from the airplane to your transportation are in a handy place (e.g. your purse or pocket).

Research limitations on belongings that you may take on the plane or into the country. For example, there are limits to how much cash you can carry. You may not be able to bring certain types of food, liquids, cell phones, or batteries. Some airlines do not allow aerosol hairspray.

Make note of relevant emergency phone numbers (e.g. police, ambulance, fire fighters) for your European country/city and put the information on your phone or in a notepad that you carry all the time

Travel Day   Pack a pashmina or light jacket in your carry-on bag in case the plane is too cold for you.

Wear comfortable shoes for the long walk from the airplane through baggage claim, passport control, and customs. Keep this long walk in mind when deciding on your carry-on luggage.

Make sure any relevant glasses and contact lens solution and case are in your carry-on bag.

Pack nuts or other dry snacks for the plane in your carry-on bag. Most airlines provide meals on international flights, but it can't hurt to carry some snacks with you. Remember that you are not allowed to carry liquids through security, but you can bring an empty water container and fill it at the gate prior to boarding the plane.

Make sure that your directions for getting from the airplane to your transportation are in a handy place (e.g. your purse or pocket).

Place your written translated request for transport to your accommodations in your purse or pocket.

Consider keeping your passport and credit cards in a passport holder worn around your neck and under your top layer of clothes. Be sure it is accessible to show the attendant at the ticket counter and the gate attendant prior to boarding the plane.

Put on your travel compression socks before take off

Upon arrival at the European airport

Claim your baggage and clear passport control and customs.

Find an ATM and get a small amount of local currency if you don't already have some. Avoid the currency exchange kiosks. Use an ATM. We usually start a trip with the equivalent of $100 in local currency. Consider immediate needs, such as, a tip for the driver of your transportation to your accommodation or buying a metro or train ticket from a ticket machine.

Car services will usually meet you in the arrivals hall. Oftentimes, train stations are located within the airport or are accessible by a connector shuttle (e.g. the Pisa People Mover). Airports usually have information kiosks in the arrivals hall. Ask questions if you are uncertain of how to find your transport from the airport to your accommodations. Also, check to see if they have free maps of the local area and/or city guide books.

ENJOY YOUR TRIP!!!

CHAPTER 12:
TRAVEL, TRIP AND INTERNATIONAL HEALTH INSURANCE

Chapter 12: Travel, Trip and International Health Insurance

- Differences among travel, trip, and international health insurance
- Beware of policy details and exclusions
- When should you shop for travel insurance?
- Finding travel and trip insurance providers that best meet your needs
- Should you buy travel insurance?
- What travel insurance does not cover
- Options for health insurance while traveling abroad

Difference between travel, trip and international health insurance

The Cigna Global website provides an excellent summary of the differences among these options. Travel insurance is designed for holidaymakers to cover cancellations, personal belongings and emergency medical

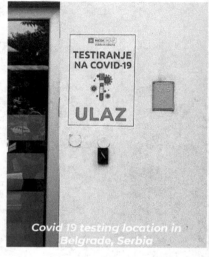

Covid 19 testing location in Belgrade, Serbia

treatment, whereas international health insurance is designed to cover inpatient treatment check-ups and continuing treatment of chronic conditions abroad.

Travel insurance is regulated by state insurance agencies. It's an actual insurance product that is underwritten by large insurance companies. It covers losses that you might face while traveling, such as car rental damage, flight delays, lost luggage, medical expenses and trip cancellation.

Trip protection is an unregulated product typically offered by a travel company or travel agency. Be careful because these plans may only cover a portion of the trip and may not reimburse you for a cancellation. Instead, you may be offered a credit or coupon for future travel. When you use online travel agencies, you will almost always be asked if you want to purchase trip insurance. Think about it carefully. If you booked a "free cancellation" stay or flight, then you probably don't need the extra trip protection.

Also, read the fine print carefully when you buy the accompanying trip insurance. We had an unpleasant experience with Lufthansa in summer 2020 when they rejected our claim for reimbursement for our tickets from Munich to Poland, stating that we should have anticipated the EU closing to Americans and not being able to fly into Munich and onward to Po-

Blue Grotto tour, Capri, Italy

land during the beginning of the coronavirus pandemic. Interestingly, part of their rationale was that we had purchased the trip insurance when we paid for our airfare. The airline didn't feel responsible, even though the insurer rejected the claim. The insurer said we should have anticipated the closing of the borders. We argued that Americans had never been denied entry to EU countries; therefore, it was not reasonable to expect us to have anticipated border closures. They eventually relented, but I was shocked that they rejected our claim in the first place.

Expatriate (international) health insurance is meant for expatriates who are living and/or working abroad for a prolonged period of time. It usually requires one to live 6 months of the year outside of one's home country. International medical insurance will usually allow you to choose where you have treatment, whereas travel insurance will usually return you back home to continue treatment once you can make the journey back.

In our case, we are too young to be eligible for Medicare so we have a health insurance policy that covers us while we're traveling as well as when we're back home in the US. We bought a Cigna Global policy for expats. It requires that we live outside of the US for 6 months of the year. That's no problem with our extensive travels. The coverage is excellent, better than any policies that we could buy through the Affordable Care Act Exchange in the US. The cost is less than the policy that we had through the Exchange (Florida Blue) and the deductible is much lower ($750 vs $15,000).

Beware of travel health policy details and exclusions

- Review the travel health insurance policy to learn whether it provides primary or secondary coverage. If it provides secondary coverage, that means all the travel medical bills first go to your primary health plan for payment. After your primary coverage, your travel insurance will pay what's left, up to the benefit limit. A better option is a primary travel health plan. It will be the first policy to pay your medical bills.

- Many travel health plans do not cover pre-existing conditions. Review the policy carefully to see how the policy defines pre-existing conditions, which may be listed as "exclusions."

- Sometimes the policy must be purchased within a certain number of days from initial trip booking. Certain things may be excluded if you book your protection later.

When should you shop for travel insurance?

Purchase your travel insurance as soon as possible. Some insurers have time limits based on the first trip planning deposit. For example, we bought travel insurance for an April 2020 trip for which an initial booking deposit was made in October 2019. Our credit card company would only provide travel insurance if the first deposit was made on the trip after January 1, 2020.

If you're taking a cruise, the cruise line typically has a 'last day to purchase' trip cancellation insurance. Airlines and online travel agencies (e.g. Expedia) also often have deadlines for purchasing cancellation insurance.

If you're planning a complex trip with lots of different transports and hotel stays, you may do better to buy one package travel insurance plan as op-

osed to paying the extra charge with each individual booking of travel or
hotel.

Be aware as you're clicking through the booking options. The extra fees
or individual trip insurance can add up and may result in greater cost than
simply buying a package plan.

Finding travel and trip insurance providers that best meet your needs

You can purchase specific types of insurance or package plans that bundle
a number of coverages into one plan. Here is a list of some of the typical
things you might look for in travel insurance:

- Baggage delay or loss
- Travel accidents
- Hazardous activity accidents
- Health insurance and medical treatment to treat injuries and illness
  while overseas
- Unexpected reoccurrence of a pre-existing medical condition
- Medical repatriation, emergency evacuation to bring you back to your
  home country in the event of illness or injury
- Accidental death and dismemberment (AD&D)
- Repatriation for death overseas to bring you back to your home coun-
  try
- Stolen or lost credit cards, passports
- Terrorism, assault
- Trip cancellation – for covered reasons or for any reason – reimbursement for insured pre-paid and non-refundable trip costs. Typical covered reasons are injury, illness, or death of you, a traveling companion,
  or family member; weather events that cause cancellations; manda-
  tory evacuations at your destination by local officials; transportation
  strikes that impact your travel; bankruptcy of your travel vendor; ter-
  rorist attacks in your destination; loss of employment for yourself or
  traveling companion
- Trip interruption

- Missed connections
- Rental car collision and liability

Tip: Before you start looking for travel insurance, identify the coverage that your credit card company is already providing for any travel that you booked using their card.

Think about your travel and which types of coverage are important to you. A good way to find policies that meet your needs is to go to a travel insurance comparison website, such as Squaremouth or TripInsurance.Com. You'll fill out a form with your travel dates, personal information, and desired insurance options. The site will provide quotes from insurers and you can choose one that best suits you.

Investopedia identified the top 3 travel insurance plans for seniors:

- Travel Guard Travel Insurance. In addition to offering standard cancellation coverage, this company features plans that cover preexisting conditions and full medical expenses.
- Travelsafe Travel Insurance
- Allianz Travel Insurance

Generally, buy trip insurance from the first day of your trip to the last. Some insurers have limits on the number of days the policy will cover. One site that I checked only provided quotes for trips that were less than 180 days in length.

Some insurance companies offer products that cover travel, trip, and international health insurance. For example, Berkshire Hathaway has plans that will protect you, your stuff and your stays, and your experience.

Policies that protect you

- Emergency Medical Insurance
- Emergency Medical Evacuation
- Accidental Death & Dismemberment
- Protecting Your Stuff and Your Stays

- Lost/Stolen Luggage
- Rental Car Coverage
- Hotel/Cruise Ship Protection
- Protecting Your Experiences
- Trip Cancellation
- Trip Interruption
- Flight Cancellation/Travel Delay
- Supplier Bankruptcy

Another important factor to consider is travel assistance. Most travel insurance plans also offer travel assistance with their policies. It's not really insurance; it's a 24/7 hotline for emergencies.

You can get online quotes for policies that are customized to your specific

	Good exactcare® value® Perfect for budget-minded travelers	Better exactcare® Great for traveling families	Different exactcare extra® Travel insurance plus inconvenience payments
Trip Cancellation	Up to 100% of trip cost	Up to 100% of trip cost	Up to 100% of trip cost ($1000 max)
Trip Interruption	Up to 100% of trip cost	Up to 150% of trip cost	150% of trip cost ($150,000 max)
Travel Delays	Up to $500	Up to $1,000	Up to $1,000
Medical Expenses	Up to $15,000	Up to $25,000	Up to $50,000
Emergency Medical Evacuation	Up to $150,000	Up to $500,000	Up to $500,000
Missed Connections	–	Up to $500	$100 (fixed)
Lost, Damaged, or Stolen Luggage	Up to $750 ($50 deductible)	Up to $1,000	$500 (fixed)
Baggage Delays	Up to $200	Up to $200	$150 (fixed)
Accidental Death & Dismemberment	–	Up to $10,000	Up to $10,000
24/7/365 Worldwide Travel Assistance	Included	Included	Included

needs. Here's a summary table of a few of Berkshire Hathaway Travel Insurance Plans. https://www.bhtp.com/travel-insurance

For a list of top rated travel insurers, see Christopher Elliott's article

https://www.forbes.com/sites/christopherelliott/2018/08/18/the-best-and-worst-travel-insurance-companies/#30bd434b4fc2

If you are seeking a visa for your travel, look up the Schengen visa insurance requirements to find a list of recommended travel insurance options:

https://www.schengenvisainfo.com/schengen-visa-insurance/

- AXA (Europe travel)
- Europ Assistance (Schengen Plus plan)
- MondialCare

Included is a chart of typical fees for travel insurance. For example, with AXA low cost insurance, you can buy a 180 day plan for 168 euros. There is also a nice article on travel insurance for seniors traveling in Europe.

Should you buy travel insurance?

Travel insurance can help you avoid unexpected expenses, just like other kinds of insurance. Options include trip cancellation or interruption, emergency medical care, and repatriation, among other things. All or part of your trip can be insured. You should consider travel and/or trip insurance if

- the financial risk is substantial, and you're worried about losing money because of a canceled trip, interrupted trip, lost bags, delayed trip, or medical emergency

- you are traveling outside of the US and want to be covered if you have any medical accidents or problems

If you can afford to lose your prepaid trip expenses, and don't mind if you do, then you probably don't need to spend the extra money for trip insurance. Also, domestic travel might not warrant the extra expense of travel insurance as your US health insurance policy or Medicare will usually cover any medical expenses. Check your policy before you travel.

For US retirees who are over 65, you may wonder if Medicare covers you while traveling abroad. The answer is usually "no." Here is what the Medicare.gov site says:

"Medicare usually doesn't cover health care while you're traveling outside the U.S. Note that Puerto Rico, the U.S. Virgin Islands, Guam, American Samoa, and the Northern Mariana Islands are considered part of the U.S. There are some exceptions, including some cases where Medicare Part B (Medical Insurance) may pay for services ...Standard Medigap Plans C, D, F, G, M, and N provide foreign travel emergency health care coverage when you travel outside the U.S. Plans E, H, I, and J are no longer for sale, but if you bought one before June 1, 2010 you may keep it."

If you have US private primary or secondary health insurance, those policies likely do not cover you while abroad either. Call your insurance provider to identify gaps in coverage that you might experience when you travel overseas.

What travel insurance does not cover

Read your policy carefully for exclusions to see if any are important to you. Typical exclusions are:

- Extreme sports where the chance of death or injury is high
- Things you do while under the influence of controlled substances
- Fear of traveling to countries, such as those listed on the State
- Department's Do Not Travel list
- Learning to fly a plane

Mushroom gnocchi lunch

- Playing professional sports
- Pregnancy
- Medical travel
- And many more

Key take-aways

1. Identify the travel insurance coverage options that you will need
2. Buy the insurance early in the trip planning process
3. For self-planned trips, consider a package plan rather than paying the extra fees for each individual travel booking trip protection
4. For tour operated trips, consider the insurance provided by the tour operator

Options for **health** insurance while traveling abroad

Medical is included in all travel insurance plans, or you can buy a stand-alone travel medical insurance policy. When you leave the US, your health insurance may not travel with you, unless you have a global plan. Whenever you are traveling abroad, get either a travel medical plan or vacation plan that includes medical emergencies.

A trip cancellation insurance plan helps you recover non-refundable costs for airline tickets, hotels, and other travel expenses in the event that you or a family member becomes ill prior to travel. It may also cover you if a disease outbreak, such as the pandemic, occurs right before you leave. As always, read the fine print for exclusions, such as pre-existing conditions, physician verification, rules about purchase dates, and the specifics of a valid "covered reason."

Medical evacuation insurance will pay for medical care and emergency evacuation in the event that you fall ill while traveling. This type of coverage could be important even if you are traveling domestically if you are traveling to remote areas.

Single-Trip travel insurance plans cover routine or emergency health care and may provide additional services, such as air ambulance, trip cancellaion and delay, and lost baggage. It's possible to find insurers that will even cover pre-existing conditions.

f you're a frequent traveler or have long-term travels, you may find that an annual travel insurance plan best meets your needs. It's generally a comprehensive plan that may cover medical emergencies or routine care for the entire year. It may also include trip cancellation and interruption. Read the fine print to learn if there is a maximum length for each trip covered, limitations to any countries visited, and length of time spent outside of

Field of Miracles, Pisa, Italy

your home country per year.

An expat insurance policy is for travelers living and working abroad. It may include expanded medical coverage, mental health, dental care, cancer treatments, chronic medical conditions, etc. You may be required to spend at least 6 months outside of your home country.

Lastly, the *International Association for Medical Assistance to Travelers* (IAMAT) is a nonprofit organization that connects travelers with English-speaking doctors around the world. Office calls and other medical visits (which you pay directly) won't cost more than a set price. Membership is free, although donations are requested.

CHAPTER 13:
CREATE A DAILY ROUTINE AND KEEP A DAILY JOURNAL

Chapter 13: Create a daily routine and keep a daily journal

- What to do?
- Develop a daily eating and exercise plan for wellness
- Strategies for shopping, buying necessities, and toting souvenirs
- Shipping items back to the US
- Keep a daily journal

What to do?

During work life, you may have noticed that each day was somewhat repetitive. You probably awakened at about the same time each day, completed a set of morning routines, like checking email, showering, dressing, and drinking coffee.

Going to work may have meant commuting to an office or shifting to your in-home office. You got through each work day doing many of the same tasks and then commuted back home. Evening commitments may have varied but, for the most part, followed a routine...maybe dinner, gym, TV, reading, sleep.

During retirement, do you find yourself creating a similar daily routine, albeit one that has more freedom and "fun"? We're creatures of habit, right? So when we travel, we may not feel comfortable just letting every day unfold willy-nilly. It may actually feel a little stressful to wake up without a plan. We're preprogrammed to want to accomplish things, to be productive, even if "productivity" is taking a walk, going to the grocery store, or visiting a museum.

We've found that daily life during our travels is more enjoyable when we have a framework for each day. In addition to adding a sense of purpose, a framework allows us as a couple to have shared expectations about the types of things that we'll do and when we'll do them. Otherwise, the day can easily devolve into a series of "what do you want to do?", "I don't know. What do you want to do?"

Initially, our daily framework looked a lot like work. Each day had to have "accomplishments," and we needed to be timely about packing in as much as we could, seeing lots of museums, historical sites, village markets, spectacular vistas, fabulous wineries. Each stop on our trip had so much to see and do. We had to make the most of it. That approach quickly exhausted us. We had definitely turned travel into work.

Over time, our daily travel routine has evolved. We've found that there are a number of small daily activities that we find enjoyable when we're traveling, and then we limit the number of "things" that we do each day to one or two major activities.

During the research and planning phase of the trip, we now make sure that we will be able to incorporate routines that make us feel comfortable, productive, and satisfied with our lives. Here are some things that we like to do every day and how we plan for them:

City park in Belgrade, Serbia

- Upon awakening, we enjoy tea or American-style coffee with lots of cream and sweetener while sitting in bed reading the news on our iPhones. During our travel planning, we ensure that our room or apartment has a refrigerator, a kettle for boiling hot water, and a nearby grocery store to purchase creamer. We bring our travel coffee mugs, a spoon, sweetener, and instant coffee and tea. We bring a voltage converter and two power adaptors so that both of our iPhones are charged while we're sleeping, ready for our morning news fix. We make sure that we have high-speed internet access in each of our accommodations.

- Exercise is really important to both of us, but we like to do different things. Brian has a morning yoga routine and exercise band workout, and then he likes to go for a bike ride. I like to go for a 3 to 4 mile walk and throw in a few strength training exercises afterwards. When we're booking accommodations, we look for easy access to walking and biking trails in nature (e.g. park, beach, mountain trail), nearby bicycle rental shops, and enough space in the accommodation to complete yoga and strength exercises.

• Being able to use public transportation is essential for us. Neither one of us likes to drive in Europe. Traffic patterns and parking can be very stressful in European towns and cities. If you stay in the historic center, parking is usually non-existent for visitors, and you frequently need a permit to even drive in these areas. During planning, we check the distance of the potential accommodation from the train and/or bus station. We prefer to travel between villages or cities using the train. Over time, we've decided that buying a continuous-use global Eurail pass offers us the most flexibility and eliminates travel hassles if we're traveling in more than one country. Otherwise, a single country train pass works well. Another pro of having a train pass is that it compels us to travel outside of our local area each day. All we have to do is hop on the train and go. Eurail has an easy to use iPhone application (RailPlanner) that helps us plan our time for departure and return.

• Limiting the number of different things that we do in a day helps us agree on what we want to do. Usually, we exercise in the morning, catch the train to somewhere, see a site, eat our main meal of the day around lunch time at a traditional local eatery, see another site, and then take the train back to our temporary home. Each evening, we typically buy greens and salad vegetables from the local market for dinner. We often take a walk after dinner and then watch Netflix or Amazon Prime on our computer or the smart TV in the accommodations.

A key point is that having a general framework helps us feel good about scheduling things that may have seemed "unproductive" during our working years, but that provide a grounding when we're frequently moving from place to place. Keep in mind, too, that, just because you're traveling ogether, it doesn't mean that you have to spend every moment together. or example, we spend an hour walking and biking separately each morning whenever possible, and then we reconvene afterwards to start our aily sightseeing.

Develop a daily eating and exercise plan for wellness

- Enjoying the local cuisine is part of the joy of traveling. Instead of limiting ourselves by eliminating certain food types (e.g. bakery items, pasta, wine, red meat), we limit the number of hours that we eat each day. This method is called time-restricted eating; we eat between 9 am and 5 pm. We are also conscious of our nutritional needs and try to eat lots of fiber – veggies, fruit, whole grains, nuts, and seeds. We usually also have one "treat" per day – a bakery item, gelato, wine, chocolate, etc.

- Another popular eating plan is a 5/2 fast where you eat for 5 days and fast for 2 days each week. If we feel like we have been overindulging, we'll incorporate fast days into our time-restricted eating routine. You can choose any 24-hour period (e.g. eating breakfast on day 1 and then no food until breakfast day 2, or, likewise, lunch to lunch, or dinner to dinner).

Tasty Italian breakfast

Always follow an eating plan that is consistent with your health and medical guidance from your physician

- For exercise, we walk a minimum of 10,000 steps per day. That may sound like a lot, but the steps are interspersed throughout the day. If

195

you have a smart phone, you can use the free health app to track your steps. We also try to incorporate some basic strength exercises every day or so (e.g. squats, lunges, push-ups, planks, abdominal crunches). You may find carrying your luggage involves the exercise of your arm and shoulder muscles. The important point is to enjoy moving and incorporate it into your daily activity. The more you move now, the longer you'll be able to move throughout your retirement years.

Strategies for shopping, buying necessities, and toting souvenirs

You can buy just about anything you need when you're in Europe. You don't need to carry it with you from the United States. You can even use Amazon in other countries. (Be sure to use the Amazon site for that country so you don't pay shipping charges from the US).

When packing, think about things that you can readily buy at your destina-

Hiking up to the fortress on Hvar Island, Croatia

tion. For example, travel with a small toothpaste, deodorant, shampoo, conditioner, shaving cream, etc., and buy a full size when you get to your European apartment. When you're traveling for a month or longer, it can be tempting to pack a full months-worth of supplements or other daily products. Think about replenishing easily purchased items on a weekly basis at the local market or pharmacy. Carrying large size products will add to the weight of your luggage.

We have a rule when we travel: If you buy it or bring it, then you have to carry it. Our rule prevents us from buying things with the expectation that the other will help us carry it from place to place.

Shipping items back to the US

If you're traveling for longer than a month, the seasons may change while you're traveling. Never fear... you can ship your seasonal clothes back to the US and buy new more seasonally appropriate clothes. We've done this numerous times. Search the Internet for UPS, DHL, or other international shipping services that are near your location. You'll need to list the items that you're shipping and perhaps pay customs fees if you have bought some of the items in Europe. Explore the option of shipping items, rather than carrying them from place to place if you find that you're accumulating "stuff."

Keep a daily journal

Chronicling your experiences is one of the best tips we have for travelers. Reviewing the fun things that you do each day will actually increase the enjoyment of the trip. Don't just let each day slip by without acknowledging the wonderful sites you visited, the interesting people you met, the tasty food and drink you enjoyed. Take the time to document what you're experiencing and appreciate those moments.

I like to keep a written journal. Brian likes to post pictures to social media, and he includes captions to help capture the experience. Either way works well to help us appreciate our adventures.

Keeping a daily journal also helps us remember places that we want to visit again...and places we don't need to see again. It also helps when we're trying to remember stories to tell friends and family. You don't have to log an entry for every day, and it doesn't have to be an extensive diary.

Here's an example of one of my trip journals:

Daily journal for 8 weeks in Italy

Day 1 Wednesday Orlando to London

The ride to the airport was uneventful. Excellent flight on Virgin Atlantic from Orlando to Gatwick in premium economy. Flat beds would have been nice, but not sure it's worth thousands more dollars on Virgin Atlantic. The food is really very good in premium. Next time though, we should try to get the bulk head...very roomy area, and they provide an ottoman for a foot rest.

Day 2 Thursday London

I was proud of our transit to the hotel. Stopped by the train ticket window to see if we needed to do anything before using our Eurail Global pass, and she told us we could just get on the train. We successfully boarded, but it was packed. Standing room only, even for the elderly woman in between us. We managed to make the 10:27 Gatwick express with a stop at Clapham Junction. With less than 10 minutes change time, we made it to the platform for the overground to Dalston Junction. We got off at Shoreditch High Street and found the hotel with the GPS. The CitizenM doesn't look like much from the outside (no signage to alert you it's there), but it's quite hip and attractive inside. Very millennial generation oriented. Self-check in on computers in a lounge/restaurant/bar/business work area. Our room was very compact, yet comfortable. Loved the bed. Wall to wall on the window end of the room with a short headboard under the window. Our room was on the 6th floor with a beautiful sky view over the neighborhood rooftops. Had lunch and dinner at the hotel. Walked quite a bit around the area and almost made our 10,000 steps for the day. Lights out around 9:45.

Day 3 Friday Beauvais, France

Got up around 6 am. Brian had a full English breakfast in the hotel, and I drank the coffee that was included in the cost. We checked out, and they called a taxi for us at 8:30 which put us very early to St Pancras station. We waited in the general lounge for over an hour for the 10:24 Eurostar. Our seats were very nice on the train and the food was delicious. Bri had quiche and I had chicken. Despite a tight connection in Gare du Nord station, we caught the 14:01 to Meru and then, unexpectedly, a bus to Beauvais. The bus dropped us off at the train station and there was a taxi stand area but no taxis. Finally called the Ibis, and fortunately one of the front desk folks spoke English, figured out our problem, and ordered a cab for us. Pascal was there to pick us up in no time. (He's going to take us to the airport tomorrow.) Checked in with no problem. Budget ground floor room...clean and comfy. Ate dinner in hotel restaurant. Turning in early to get ready for a full day tomorrow.

Day 4 Saturday Lucca

We had breakfast in the hotel. Pascal picked us up at 10:30 and the airport was a quick 10 minute drive. We printed our boarding passes prior to leaving home, so we walked straight to security. They checked our bag sizes, and we were good to go with our back packs and personal items. Ryanair proved to be quite efficient. They boarded the plane from the tarmac and used both the front and back of plane doors. We took off on time and landed 25 minutes early in Pisa. Finding the PisaMover was easy (followed the big signs). Payment machines are right before the gates...5 euros each. We got off at the second and final stop, found our train to Lucca which was at the farthest possible track, and enjoyed the 45 minute ride. Even though I wrote down the directions to the apartment, we got lost and ended up using GPS. Arrived a little after 4. Mrs. Sonia provided a quick intro to the apartment, which was somewhat sufficient. We used the Internet to learn how to use the appliances. Many shops were already closed, however, we were able to find a grocery store. Dinner was at Il Coure... lasagna for me and a fish dish for Bri in a tomato sauce.

Day 5 Sunday Lucca

We wandered around town. Checked on Bri's bike rental, but the one he wanted was rented by a Dutch couple all day. Found a grocery store. Late lunch at Puccini's Museum Cafe (pizza and pasta) and then reading before bed.

Day 6 Monday Lucca

Brian picked up his rental bike at 9 and then we set off for our first trek around the wall. Lovely morning. The rest of the day was relaxing with several small walks around town, more grocery shopping, lunch at a restaurant near the amphitheater area.

Day 7 Tuesday Lucca

We woke up early to enjoy a walk/bike around the wall before the cooking class. Unfortunately, the organizer put us on the wrong date so we rescheduled for Wednesday. Lunch was at Restaurante All' Oliva ... I had meat tortelli with a bolognese sauce and Bri had veal with mashed pota-toes. We indulged in chocolate cake and gelato for dessert. After a rest in the afternoon, we walked around the town for a while in the early evening. Dinner was a light salad at home. Finally figured out how to turn on Netflix on the TV and started watching Reign. Not wowed by it, but it's some en-tertainment for the evening.

Day 8 Wednesday Lucca

First thing this morning, I walked the wall while Brian did his yoga here. At 9:30, the cooking class chef — Giuseppe — met our class of 7 near Il Coure, and we meandered through the city, stopping at shops and a mar-ket to pick up various items for the meal we would make. The other stu-dents were interesting... an accountant (Linda) from Laguna Hills with her daughter (Andrea) and niece (Jennifer), a young retired chemical engineer (Young) who worked for Merck, and a clinical trial researcher (Jason) from NYC who is taking a holiday break between jobs. Brian was a star student and helped the chef manage the cooking duties and cleaning. I spent more time talking with the other students. We sat next to Young at lunch and made plans to have lunch with her and her husband on Friday. They've been retired 10 years, are 60 years old, and have been leading a nomadic life since retiring from their jobs in New York City. Her husband, however, got bored so he is teaching during fall semester in S Korea and is also writ-ing a textbook on engineering explosions. After such a fabulous lunch, we had a light dinner of cheese, meat, bread, and honey from Giuseppe 's grandfathers olive orchard/farm.

Day 9 Thursday Lucca

We awoke early again so we could walk/bike the wall before Chiara stopped by. The dryer aspect of the washing machine is still a mystery. Chiara said the left hand side of the controls were dryer cycles but she's not right. I tried the mixed cycle, and it rewashed my wet clothes. I will need to read more information on the Internet. It was a relaxing, lazy day. Lunched at Trattoria de Leo, just down the street.

Then napped and read. Went out for a walk to the grocery store in late afternoon. Dinner was a light salad at home. Young told us about a free organ concert at San Martino cathedral. It was lovely, but the church was hot and the pews were very hard on the bum. We stayed for about an hour, which worked out well as we saw a spectacular evening sky when we emerged from the church.

Day 10 Friday Lucca

No plans in the morning so we slept in til 7. A little rain delayed our walk. We had lunch at Trattoria de Julia with Young and her husband, Robert. Greatly enjoyed the meal and the company. They have been location in-dependent for 10 years after retiring at age 50. For three years, they lived in a conversion van and traveled Europe. They're looking to buy a house in Italy now. They say southern Italy is very affordable. After lunch, we all walked to the market for groceries and then parted ways. Relaxed, and then watched some Reign the rest of the day.

Day 11 Saturday Lucca

Went on our morning walk/bike ride around the wall. Then we explored more of the town. Walked to the Italian School, found the bus station, me-andered around a bit, and then had lunch at a restaurant that was tucked back off the street in a court yard like area...mainly a parking area, but enough room for a number of outdoor tables. Did laundry and relaxed the rest of the day. We were awoken around 11 pm by a percussion band, right outside our building. They played for about 20 minutes (quite loudly). Wish we had gotten up and taken a video.

Day 12 Sunday Lucca

walked around the wall and Bri took the morning off. Figured out how to wash/dry the sheets. Took the 12:45 train to Montecatini for lunch. We found a very cute restaurant close to the train station. We planned to go up to Montecatini Alto but a thunderstorm rolled in while we were eating. Luckily, the rain broke in time for us to walk back to the train station and catch the 14:52 back to Lucca. We stopped by the grocery store on the way home from the train station. Had salad for dinner and watched Reign before heading to bed to read a while.

Day 13 Monday Lucca

Woke up early to get a walk in before our first day of Italian class, but I lost my motivation. Bri went for a bike ride. Good Italian class. There are five students—Nikki from Australia, Jerry from Dorchester, Kathy from Boise, and us. Eva is our teacher, and she is from Lucca. We learned how to introduce ourselves and some verb conjugations. Ate lunch at a restaurant in the amphitheater. Bri liked it better than I did. It was more tourist-oriented and pricier than other places. After lunch, took a nap and then went for a walk/bike around the wall. Dinner was a light salad at home. Watched a couple of Reigns and then read for a while.

Day 14 Tuesday Lucca

Woke up early and went for walk/bike ride around wall. Did laundry, then headed out for our Italian lessons. Class was informative with lots of learning about personal info statements...I am from, I'm married, my family consists of, etc. also learning how to conjugate common verbs. Had lunch at Trattoria Gigi with Young and Robert. They're leaving Thursday to go back to Seoul. Robert, turns out, will not be teaching this fall. Stopped by the Conard City grocery afterward. That's definitely the best supermarket. Took a nap after all that. Enjoyed a short walk and minimal dinner in the evening. Watched Reign and read before bed.

Day 15 Wednesday Lucca

Awoke at 5 am, had coffee, and then went for walk around the wall at 7. We left for Italian class around 8:50, stopped by a cafe for sandwiches for our 11 am break, and continued on our way. Class started at 9:15. Jerry and Kathy are on a different track and left for an excursion to Livorno at 10:15. Nikki, Brian, and I wrote short stories about our lives, learned more verbs, and practiced our numbers. After class, Bri and I had a very marginal lunch at Osteria XXXX. It's the first time I've had a lasagna that I didn't like. Brian's chicken scallopini was undercooked. We ate little so we stopped for pastries on the way home. Very yummy. After a rest, we walked/rode on the wall a bit more. Dinner was a light salad. Enjoyed watching Reign while we washed clothes.

A positive about this week is that the crowds are much thinner. It's easier to maneuver around bikes, runners, and walkers on the wall and in the city. If we come back, it would be better to wait until the last week in August. Much more pleasant.

Day 16 Thursday Lucca

Awoke early and went on walk before class. Had lunch at Gigi's again... very yummy...pasta for me. We napped and then went back to school for a cooking class at 4. Lots of fun. About 20 participants. We made ravioli, pork ribs, biscotti, and a side dish veggie. Lots of wine and nice company through the evening. Got home around 9.

Day 17 Friday Lucca

Awoke around 7 and got ready for school. It was our last day so Bri and I stopped by the grocery store on the way and bought pastries for everyone. We said goodbye to Eva at 1 and then Jerry, Nikki, Bri, and I went to a cute restaurant in San Francesca piazza. Had a lovely lunch. Napped when we got home and lounged for the rest of the evening.

Day 18 Saturday Lucca

Woke up early and walked around the wall. Took the train to Montecatini Terme, walked to the funicular, and went up to Montecatini Alto. It's a quick ride in a cog rail type train with slatted wooden seats and old wooden windows. The train has been in operation since 1898. The views on the way up are lovely. Next time, we need to be sure to stand on the outer back deck for unobstructed pictures/views. Midway, the train coming down passes. At the top, the village is lovely, dating to the 1500s, I believe. A sign said that the village was sacked by Cosemo Medici and the clock tower is the oldest remaining original structure. One of the churches was founded by the carmelites, which is interesting because Brian's church in Herrin is our lady of Mt Carmel. We lit candles for Mom and JC.

It was an extremely hot day so we only walked around for about 45 minutes, then took the funicular back down. We stood on the upper outer deck with several other people, every seat was full. Back in Montecatini Terme, we walked to a restaurant near the train station, same as where we ate last Sunday. It's called Centrale. Food is excellent and service is quite nice. We caught the 13:52 train back to Lucca and walked home from the train station. After a rest, I called Lisa and chatted for about 45 minutes. Then we went to the Conad City grocery store. Watched Reign and read before bed.

Day 19 Sunday. Lucca

We slept in until 7 this morning, read the news on our phones, drank coffee, and then went for our walk/ride on the wall. After washing the sheets and showering, I made train plans for the upcoming week. We'll visit a nearby village or city each day. We left for lunch at Osteria Cantine Bernardini. It's one of the oldest restaurants in Lucca — 1586! We ate inside, downstairs, in what might have been a wine cellar of the Bernardini palace. Food was delicious. Service was excellent. Would definitely go back again. Especially loved the bag of bread they brought to the table. Since it was in a bag, I brought a couple of pieces home. Lounged for the rest of the afternoon. Had an arugula salad with tomato and Parmigianino for dinner. Watched Reign and then read before bed.

A couple of observations...we really like being able to walk and ride each morning. That will be important as we identify future home bases on our trips. We also like being close to the train station. Probably don't need a continuous rail pass. We should estimate how many days we'll actually travel and see if that costs less.

Day 20 Monday (Labor Day back in the States). Lucca

Woke up early, had coffee, then walked the wall. We set out for the train station around 10 am. Stopped for a pastry before leaving the old city gates. Took the 10:30 train to Viareggio. I normally plan where to go and how to get there, but didn't this time. We took a guess at the direction of

204

the beach and started walking. We happened upon a large park with vendors set up under the trees, various play areas for kids, and a number of bicycle rentals. We rented two bikes and set off down the busy paved path through the park. The trees were lovely and provided nice shade on a hot day. The breeze from riding the bike also helped with the heat. When the park path ended, we turned left and found a bike path near and parallel to the beach. It was narrow and a tight squeeze for more than one bike, which made me nervous every time a bicycle passed going the opposite way. That path lead to a set of bathing houses with tons of beach chairs, changing rooms, etc. A flea market was set up on the boardwalk on the street side of the promenade. Crowded. Hot. We parked our bikes and walked around just a bit. Getting back on the bikes, we turned the other direction on the bike path and eventually found a very broad promenade with more upscale shops, restaurants, and bathing houses. Lots of chairs for rent on the beach here as well. There must be thousands of beach chairs along the shore.

We returned the bikes in the park and walked back down to the promenade to find a restaurant. Brian ordered a disgusting octopus dish and I had ravioli. After lunch, we wandered back to the station, caught the train heading towards Firenze, and made our way back home. Stopped by the Pam grocery store. Relaxed at home for the rest of the afternoon and evening. Watched Reign, read my book.

For Viareggio...one visit is probably enough. It's a busy beach town, more modern than quaint. The park was nice, and we liked that we could rent bikes and give Bri a break from the walking.

Day 21 Tuesday Lucca

Skipped the walk on the wall this morning and headed for Pisa around 10:30. It's a quick train ride. We got off at Pisa S Rossore since it's closest to the leaning tower. Getting out of the station, we followed the 'uscita' signs and then the 'Torre Pendente' signs. Take a left out of the station and walk down Via Andrea Pisano until you reach the gate to the field of miracles. It only took us about 5 minutes. Once through the gate, we walked down to the ticket office on the right hand side of the pedestrian walk/street. They aren't very informative when you buy tickets. We bought tickets to the tower for 11 am (18 euros each) and the baptistry (5 euros each; entrance anytime). No other instructions were provided. We made our way to the tower line and learned that you can't carry bags (purses, backpacks, etc) up the tower. There's a free cloakroom in the orange building near the tower. Go stand in cloakroom line, hold your tower ticket... a woman escorts you quickly to a locker, she hands you a plastic card and marks your ticket with the locker number. Be sure to keep your phone/camera with you if you want to take pictures. There's a public pay bathroom near the cloakroom in the same orange building.

The leaning tower is about 250 steps up and then, of course, back down. There's a platform at the top that has one-way traffic around the circumference. Another narrow set of stairs goes up to the bells. I found it particularly scary...very narrow, high, and disconcerting with the tilt. The trip all the way back down was okay. The woman in front of me was scared and very cautious, and I was glad for her slow pace. We high fived each other when we reached the bottom. No need for shared language on that one.

Once on the ground level, Bri and I decided to walk through the historic city center to find a place for lunch. There are a number of sidewalk cafes just off the field of miracles but we wanted something less crowded and less touristy. We walked through the cafes, by the university and then through an upscale shopping area and then crossed the river at the Piazza Garibaldi. In the area across the bridge is a set of stairs leading down to free public bathrooms. They were less than clean, had no toilet paper, and only one women's closet was open. It's an option if desperate. Turned left after that temple looking building, walked a block, and turned right into a tucked away square. Had lunch at a cute, quiet family operated place tucked away in the small square off the main road.

After lunch, we crossed the bridge, turned left, and walked down the busy road to Ave San Maria, just before the next bridge. Walked by many university of Pisa (founded in 1343) buildings on Ave San Maria back to the field of miracles. We stopped in the baptistry before making our way to the train station for the 14:42 train to Lucca. There is a public bathroom at the train station but it's another only-if-desperate option. Once back in Lucca, we found a pharmacy for Bri to buy cream for the rash on the back of his ankle. The pharmacist was very helpful. I also bought some lip balm.

he rest of the evening was relaxing. Salad for dinner. Reign and then read-
ng before bed.

Day 22 Wednesday Lucca

kipped the walk on the wall again and took off for Florence around 9.
uckily, we remembered how to get to the Duomo from last year's trip. It's
nost expeditious to turn left out of the gate, walk to the station exit and
ake the stairs down to the underground passageway. Stay left, then go
traight. There's a public pay bathroom about ½ way through the tunnel
1 euro). There's also a very clean public pay bathroom (0.80 euros) at the
ear of the McDonalds which is on the left as you're exiting the station.

At the end of the tunnel, there are two possibilities: a set of stairs going
up to street level and a passage to the left. Take the left passage and then
valk up the stairs to street level. Go straight across the street and keep

valking for several blocks. Just stay
traight and you'll see the Duomo
and baptistery. There's a public pay
bathroom on one side of the square.
We haven't been inside the cathedral or baptistery yet. There are ex-
remely long lines. Found out that
you have to make a reservation in advance. We tried to attend mass last
year and there was a mob of people
that we opted to avoid.

To get to the Ponte Vecchio bridge,
walk between the cathedral and baptistery and continue straight down
the very busy street. You'll end up in
the Piazza de la Signoria...see the replica of David in front of the Pallazzo
Vecchio. Across the square, see the covered area with lots of statues. Walk
past it and to the right. The Uffizi Galleria is on your right. Walk up the
steps to the street and turn right to get to the bridge.

We had lunch at a cute place with a patio tucked off the street behind the main restaurant. A couple overhead us talking about Chicago pizza and asked where we were from. Turned out, they were young newlyweds from Overland Park on their honeymoon. Nick and Natalie. We bought them lunch to celebrate their marriage and they joined us for our trip to the Boboli gardens in the Pitti Palace.

To get to the Pitti Palace, cross over the Ponte Vecchio bridge and keep walking straight for about 3 blocks. It's on the left on the hill. The gardens are worth seeing. Great views. Porcelain museum at top of garden with serving pieces from 1700-1800s. If you walk down the hill from the porcelain museum, there's a nice public bathroom on the left. The palace is also nice, but similar to furnishings and art in other palaces. Worth seeing if you haven't toured many palaces. There's a nice cafe and clean restroom. The restroom is a bit of a walk downstairs and a long hallway.

We made it back to the station for the 15:10 to Viareggio. It was about an hour and a half to Lucca. Stopped in our favorite vegetable market on the walk home from the station. Filled our water bottles at the fountain. Enjoyed salad for dinner. Watched Reign and read before bed.

Day 23 Thursday Lucca

We both took to the wall early this morning and enjoyed the sparse crowd. Brian likes riding through the city streets, when minimal people are out and about. This was the first slightly cool morning...about 60 degrees... and I enjoyed wearing a long sleeve workout top for a change. We decided to stay in Lucca for the day. Grocery shopped in the morn at Conad City. Lunch was at a cute place off of Fillunga, very nearby...L'isola che non c'era. Food was delicious but we had the odd experience of tipping a couple of street musicians who came to the tables, collected money from everyone, then played less than one song before moving on. We felt gypped.

Then we walked to the museum that describes the Via Francigena pilgrimage —Canterbury to Rome. Entrance is 5 euros each. Nice restrooms on the second floor. There are several video, audio, and interactive displays. We liked the one that let you pick out a typical meal and then told you how well prepared you were nutritionally for the next leg of the journey. There was also a neat path in the floor that you could walk on with a back pack that gave you an estimate of how long it would take you to complete the pilgrimage. We wandered around town some more and then came home for a salad for dinner. Watched Reign and read before bedtime.

Day 24 Friday. Lucca

Supposed to be a rainy day so we stayed in Lucca. Turned out that it sprinkled off and on. I walked the wall and washed clothes. Bri and I went to the grocery store and then tried to make peanut butter cookies in a skillet on the stove. It didn't work out. We went to lunch at the Osteria San Giorgio down the street. We noticed the there is an estitica next door which turns out to be a place for pedicures and massages. Bri and I are signed up for Tuesday morning appointments. We spent the afternoon wandering around a bit. Found the immigration museum but it wasn't open. Dinner was a salad. Watched Reign, planned our day trip to La Spezia, and then read before bed.

Day 25 Saturday Lucca

We caught the 7:59 am train to Viareggio and then on to La Spezia. The train into La Spezia was packed and so was the station. It was easy to find our way down to the marina— followed the signs. The town is sizable and the walk to the marina goes through a very nice pedestrian area. We passed by several streets with steps heading straight up the cliff. One of them takes you to the castle. We'll go see it on Friday when we return for an overnight. We decided to stay in La Spezia one night prior to Riomaggiore after seeing how quaint the town seems. Found a nice affordable hotel a couple of blocks from the station.

Adjacent to the marina is a lovely park. It looks like a good area for bicycling. There's a park and then a long wide promenade along the harbor. As you enter the marina, free public bathrooms are on the right next to the Pescheria. We walked down the promenade to the ticket booth and bought 2 one-way tickets to Riomaggiore....18 euros each. The ferry ride took about an hour and provided a very scenic ride. Stopped in Portovenere on the way. Very charming village with a beautiful church built in the 11th century sitting on the cliff at the point. Rounding the point, we traveled up the coast. There are a number of small clusters of homes. No idea how people access the homes. They appear to sit on the side of the hills with no obvious roads or pathways. The boat narration said one home had 1000 steps with no handrails connecting it to an upper road.

The 'dock' in Riomaggiore is a set of rocks with concrete steps leading up to the village. It was very crowded. Tons of families with kids, dogs large and small...chaotic. We sat down at a street side restaurant but left before ordering when a couple sat down at the table adjoining ours with a very large furry dog. Dining with large animals is not something I've gotten used to yet. There also seemed to be a lot of flies around the tables. We left and walked up to the end of the pedestrian zone. After turning around, we walked down and found a very cute restaurant...La Cantina del Macellaio... where we ate inside at a back table near the air conditioning. The owner is American from Brooklyn and has been there 20 years. Spoke beautiful Italian and, of course, perfect English. Brian had a delicious polenta dish and I had ravioli.

The owner gave us directions to the train station. We walked down the hill and turned right into a pedestrian tunnel that was several blocks long. It ended at the train station. Only two tracks. We waited at track 1 for the train to La Spezia. The ride was maybe 10 minutes. In La Spezia, we wandered around for about 20 minutes, found a promising hotel for Friday, and then went back to await our train. Everything went smoothly getting back to Lucca, although the train to Pisa was quite warm. Once back in Lucca, we stopped at our favorite pastry shop for waters and a juice for Bri. It was about 5:30 when we got home. Watched Reign and read before bed.

Day 26 Sunday. Lucca

It was raining when we woke up. Lovely thunderstorm actually. Things cleared up around 8:30 and we went for our walk/bike ride around 9. We finally went to the immigration museum. It was all in Italian so we didn't understand much, but the pictures were interesting. Brian can now tell Ernesto that we visited the museum. After that, we went to a cute restaurant tucked away in one of the side streets. A Viking tour group passed by while we ate so it must have been on the way to a tourist site. After lunch, we walked down Fillungo, looking at the shops and jostling among all the tourists. Weekends are definitely busy in the old city. We went home for a bit and then back out for another walk. Dinner was a salad. Watched Reign and read.

Day 27 Monday Lucca

We left for Florence on the 8:30 train and arrived around 10:30. It's nice visiting now that we know the city a little better. We walked up to the Duomo area and cut over to the river through side streets. Crossed the Ponte Vecchio and turned left to find our way up to the panoramic viewing spot and church. We turned up too early and walked up a very steep street to arrive at an old fort. We followed the wall of the Pitti Palace. The fort was closed. An older gentleman in his car was talking to a couple of other men. He told us the museum was closed and asked where we were wanting to go. We told him the viewing area and he said it was 4 km away, but he could drive us for just the cost of gas. We got in the car and sure enough

it was a good distance. Glad we had a ride. We paid him 10 euros for his kindness. We revisited the church first, walked through part of the cemetery, stopped at the public pay bathroom, and headed past the next church to the viewing area. Florence is really lovely with the mountains in the background and river running through it. Brian took a number of pictures. We took a more direct walking path straight down to the river area. The key is to cross at the next bridge, not the Ponte Vecchio. Crossing the bridge, we ended up close to the Duomo area. We saw another spectacular

View from the Castello San Giorgio, La Spezia, Italy

church that had a lovely noon hour bell ringing. After that we found a nice sidewalk restaurant and ate lunch. Unfortunately, there were little gnats that kept flying into our wine and food, really bothersome. After eating, we headed back to the train station, caught the 13:38, and made it back to Lucca by 3:30. We stopped in our favorite veggie market. Frittata and salad stuff for dinner. Reign and reading before bed.

Day 28 Tuesday Lucca

Woke up about 6:30 and puttered around until my pedicure appointment at 9. Brian had a massage at 10. Both were good. Only cost $88 total for both and the place was right across from our apartment on San Giorgio. We tipped 4 and 5 euros. After Bri's massage, we went to buy tickets to tonight's Puccini concert and then walked around a bit, stopped by the ATM, went to lunch at Gigi's and then bought groceries at Conad. That's probably our last grocery run before we leave on Friday. Watched a Reign when we got home and then took a nap. Had a salad for dinner and then left for the Puccini concert at 6:20 to get there early for a good seat.

Day 29 Wednesday Lucca

Enjoyed the day in Montecatini Terme. Saw the thermal park. Ate lunch at a beautiful place overlooking the main square.

Day 30 Thursday Lucca

Spent our last day in Lucca

Day 31 Friday La Spezia

Checked out of our Lucca apartment a day early to spend a little more time in Liguria. Took the train to Viareggio then on to La Spezia. Our room at the Hotel Venezia wasn't ready yet when we arrived but they let us leave our bags. Wandered around La Spezia. Walked up the stairs to the old castle. Bought the ticket to the castle and museum. I think we had seen too many museums by then and enjoyed the walk around the castle more than the museum. Wandered back down the stairs to the pedestrian zone then to the park and harbor. Had lunch at a nice restaurant...Hosteria Chicchetterla ...in one of the squares. Checked into our hotel. Rested and then wandered some more and had dinner at a small place along a side street.

Day 32 Saturday Riomaggiore

Ve ate breakfast in the hotel, a nice continental spread with a wonder-ul coffee machine. I had 4 cappuccinos. When we checked out, the clerk old us the breakfast was complimentary. Very nice. Caught the train to iomaggiore. Waited about 20 minutes to meet our hotel host at 11:30. he walked us to our room, which wasn't ready yet, but she let us leave our bags. The room is simple, spacious, includes a sitting area, table with hairs and place settings, and a balcony overlooking the town and sea. We valked all over Riomaggiore...up to the church and castle, up to the top of he town, back down to the train station. Had lunch at a very small, cute estaurant adjacent to our building. Rested after lunch. Took the train to Manarola in the late afternoon. Stopped by the market to pick up cheese, neat, crackers, wine, and beer for dinner. Enjoyed eating on the balcony vatching the crowds from above. The view was stunning. Lovely evening.

Day 33 Sunday. Riomaggiore

Woke up at 5 to get ready, drink coffee on the balcony, and be at the Bar Stazione to pick up our breakfast by 8. Turns out, we rushed for no reason. The ferry arrived about 9 and tickets weren't open until a few minutes before. Luckily, this early ferry wasn't crowded. We sat up top and en-oyed the non-stop ride to Monterosso..about 30 minutes. The 'dock' was similar to Riomaggiore, a concrete platform on the rocks. The town is more walkable and much larger than Riomaggiore. Lots of cute restaurants and shops, some hotels. More upscale. You could ride a bike if you wanted. It's split in two with a smaller half at the ferry dock side. We walked around that side first, found the path curving up and over to the other side, and took the steep steps/path up to a church and capuchin monastery that has been there since 1618. A plaque commemorating the 400th anniversary provided the founding info. It consists of a lovely church with a beautiful cemetery above it at the peak of the hill. Wandering back down, we briefly explored the larger beach front portion of the village, bought Bri a t-shirt, and then headed to the next town, Vernazza.

Vernazza is very quaint. It was the town we visited in 2008 during our 10th anniversary Mediterranean cruise. It's a little flatter and more walkable than Riomaggiore, smaller than Monterosso. We saw people riding bikes, but it didn't look wise. There's a trail leading to Corniglia, not sure how easy a trek that would be. We wandered around the town to the seaside.

It was packed with tour groups. Restaurants in the main square open a noon. Lots of people were waiting. We wandered back up the hill. Spen some time looking for a bathroom. There is apparently only one public toi let...1 euro or free with Cinque Terre park pass. It's located at one end o the #2 train platform. Ate lunch at a less hectic place right below the trair station. Caught the 13:14 train back to Riomaggiore.

Stopped at the market for fruit and deli meat to have for dinner and ther rested in our room while the crowds inundated the town.

Day 34 Monday. Sorrento

Traveled all day to Sorrento from Riomaggiore.

Riomaggiore to Levistra ... train was delayed

Then to Roma Termini...missed connection, but rebooking was easy

Then to Naples Centrale

Then on the Circumvetsuvious to Sorrento. What a crazy ride. The train was absolutely packed. Sorrento is the last stop. We asked a taxi driver about taking us to the hotel and I think he said it would be about 30 euros. It was only about a mile so we walked all the way through town to the hotel. At least things were familiar from last year's trip. We turned down a set of steps just past the hospital. We found the parking area but had a hard time finding the front of the hotel. We finally entered the back door and wandered to the front desk. The room was spacious but dated. Comfortable. Ulisse Deluxe Hostel.

We walked down the street to dinner in Marina Grande. Cute restaurant with excellent service, right on the road/boardwalk. It wasn't as busy or fancy as some of the places, but we were very happy with our meals. Walked back up the curving old walkway to the upper town and then found our way back to the hotel.

Day 35 Tuesday

The hotel breakfast was a good bargain...10 euros each and it included hot items—eggs, etc—as well as many pastries, meats, cheeses. The coffee machine was a real plus. It was nice to have good coffee and I had several cups.

The hotel called a taxi to take us to the Piccola Marina ferry dock. We bought tickets on the 11:10 fast ferry. It was huge, plenty of room for the masses of people waiting with us on the dock. The trip took about ½ hour. Getting off in Capri Marina Grande was a little chaotic. We waited in line at a place on the dock called bus central. It turned out that the bus didn't go to Anacapri, only Capri, so we had to walk down the road to the right for a couple of blocks to find the correct bus. It was with the funicular. We bought two tickets (5 euros) and stood in line for about 30 more minutes. Finally, a woman walked up to the line and said she had 13 seats if anyone wanted to pay 5 euros per person. We took two of the seats and were very thankful to be making our way up the mountain. The bus dropped us at the Piazzale near our B&B, then we walked up a narrow pathway for about ½ mile. Signs were posted regularly to let us know we were on the right track.

The B&B is lovely with beautiful grounds, a large lovely terrace, and a nice size room with a jetted bath tub. After settling in, we walked into town for lunch at Caffe Michel Angelo...Luciana's brother's restaurant. After wandering a bit, we stopped in the market, bought some things for a light dinner, and went back to the B&B. After a rest, we walked along the upper paved path for quite a distance towards the philosophers park. Lovely homes, gardens along the way.

Dinner was wine, meat, cheese, and crackers. We watched a Reign and read before bed.

Day 36 Wednesday

The B&B breakfast, served from 8:30-10:30, was a lovely continental spread with bread, meat, cheese, yogurt, fruit, etc. After breakfast, we followed the paved path above the B&B into Anacapri and then onward to the Villa San Michele. It's a beautiful villa, just before the Phoenician Steps with amazing gardens and views. An old chapel on the property was converted to a small music venue. There's a sphinx from Egypt that is thousands of years old. We took pictures and touched it. Need to find out the significance of touching it. The house had one bedroom, a kitchen, dining room, office, living room and then lots of garden area with a few other small buildings. A professional photo shoot with a glamorous male model was taking place while we wandered through.

After the villa, we decided to walk down the Phoenician steps—921 stone steps--- to Capri...quite a walk. The views were gorgeous and it's one of those things that you must do on the island. We saw a number of people walking up. We were happy that we chose to walk down. When we reached the main Piazza in Capri, it was very crowded and we looked for a restaurant out of the main fray. Our choice was on the third floor overlook-

ing the piazza and the sea. It was a delicious lunch with excellent service.

After lunch, we decided to finish the trek by walking to Villa Jovis, former villa of Tiberius in 29 AD. He ruled the Roman Empire from there for 11 years. Somehow we took a wrong turn and ended up at the natural arch, which was beautiful, but not near the Villa. We backtracked and found the correct path. The climb up to the Villa was fairly steep, but on a well paved path. There's a toilet about ⅔ of the way up and also right at the top, just before the ticket booth for the park. The ruins are impressive and involve lots more climbing and steps. There's a point called Tiberius Jump where people were thrown off the cliff as punishment for crimes. It's a very long way down to the ocean.

The walk back to Capri is all downhill thankfully. Once there, we easily found the bus to Anacapri and made our way home...over 19,000 steps on our health data app. For dinner, we walked across the street to the agritourismo restaurant for dinner. We arrived at 6:30 and learned that dinner is at 8. No matter, they served us wine and bruschetta, then brought the caprese salad, followed by spaghetti pomodore, then a large plate of meats—rabbit, chicken, steak, and sausage. We could hardly eat any of the meat after all of the other courses. Dessert was a plate of various fruits. We met a young Canadian couple during dinner and chatted with them all evening. Kendra and Stephen. They are currently between jobs, but living in London on a 2-year visa for young people in the British empire. They plan to find jobs and go back to work when they return to London.

By the time we paid the check it was a little after 11 pm. The experience was actually very reasonable... 108 euros and we gave Luigi 120 euros. Would definitely do the whole thing again the next time we're in Anacapri.

Day 37 Thursday

We started the day with breakfast. Luciano gave us some recommendations for spending the day. She also said to contact her directly through email or WhatsApp if we come back and she can give us a much better price on accommodations. Also, she can find us an apartment if we want to stay longer.

There are some Roman ruins near the Blue Grotto that were hypothetically within walking distance. We took off through the town, heading

Temple at Paestrum, Italy

downhill all the way to the blue grotto area but somehow missed the entrance. By the time we got there, it was pouring rain and we didn't have umbrellas. Fortunately, we came upon the bus stop and a bus picked us up within about 10 minutes. Thank goodness, because the walk back uphill would have been grueling as well as dangerous with the car traffic on the main road. We tipped the bus driver for his exemplary navigation of tight squeezes with other vehicles. There was a lot of vituperative chatter among drivers as we made our way back up the hill with frequent stops to squeeze by with nothing but an inch to spare. Once back in Anacapri, we found a cute pizzeria to eat inside. After, we walked back home, stopping by the grocery for items for a light dinner. After a rest, we walked down to the philosophers park to see the stunning views of the lighthouse and then the Belvedere walk to see the three rocks off the coast.

Dinner was ham, cheese, crackers, and wine on the patio with a cloudy, but still pretty onset of dusk.

Day 38 Friday,

Traditional Apulian dry-stone huts Trulli houses -- in Alberobello, Italy

It was a cooler, windy morning so we sat under the cover in the breakfast area. Luciana served us and talked with us while we ate. Paola, (her son?), took us to the ferry for 25 euros at 9:15. It was worth every penny. We boarded the 9:35 ferry which actually departed close to 10. At the port, we caught a taxi to the train station for 15 euros, which again was worth every penny. Naples is nuts. So much traffic and it was extra hectic because the Italian president was visiting Naples. At the train station, we purchased first class tickets on the fast train to Paestrum. We sat with a French family (parents and adult daughter) that we ended up sharing a taxi with in Paestrum. We arrived at our hotel around 2 pm.

The hotel in Paestrum was very charming, just lovely old villa with comfortable lounge areas and dining room. Our room was spacious, but not very quiet and a little too warm even with the air conditioning.

We walked around the archeological park...awesome temples...and then went back for a rest. We wanted to eat dinner around 6:00, but had a hard time finding a place that served dinner before 7:30.

Day 39 Saturday

The hotel breakfast was fabulous but we had to eat quickly for an 8 am taxi pickup. We caught the 8:50 train to Battapaglia, then to Taranto, then Brindisi, then Lecce. Took a taxi from the train station to the hotel. We were a little worried because the taxi driver was an older woman who didn't speak any English. I showed her the print out with the hotel name and address. She managed to find it after a phone call for directions...about 12 euros for about a mile. Taxis are not cheap. We arrived about 4:45. Went to eat. Found a cute place that served during the early pre-dinner hours. We talked with a couple from Rotterdam for quite some time, then walked back through the old town to home.

The hotel is quite lovely...modern elegance. Our room has a beautiful walled patio, just for us with dense foliage and flowers peeping through and above the balustrades of the wall.

Bolzano, Italy

Day 40 Sunday

The B&B breakfast was wonderful, a nice spread of pastries. Meat, cheese, juices. We spent the day roaming around, trying to find the sites on our visit-a-City guide. We bought a ticket to see 4 churches. The Duomo was included... quite spectacular. Below the crypt, there's an excavation area where you can see skulls and other bones. No pictures allowed. We ate lunch al fresco at a cute restaurant. Brian enjoyed a chick pea soup. I had salad and fries. All the meals are becoming blurred together. We rested in the afternoon and then had dinner at the nearby caffe. We made the mistake of ordering two aperitivo plates (only 6 euros each) and it was so much food that we gave one plate to the young people sitting next to us.

Day 41 Monday

Breakfast at the hotel was lovely. Valentina picked us up for our 8-hour tour of the area at 9:30. We visited Brindisi, Alberobello, Monopolie. The trulli houses in Alberobello were very charming and there were tons of them interspersed throughout the town and countryside. We had lunch in the middle of the trulli part of town. Lots of veggies and bread for antipasti. We opted to skip the main meal and pasta...too full. The seaside towns were beautiful with buildings on cliffs leading straight down to the ocean. The cliffs are full of caves at sea level. The water was a beautifu blue. Vale dropped us off in Lecce at 5:30 and we walked straight to the caffe near our hotel.

Day 42 Tuesday

The taxi picked us up at 5:15 for the 6:06 am train to Bologna and then a train to Bolzano. It was a long day riding the train, but everything went smoothly and we arrived in Bolzano with no problems. Our apartment is centrally located, has a nice restaurant attached, and was quiet for sleep-

Cuggiono, Italy

ing. We had dinner at the gasthaus ristorante...Bri had a typical German sausage, sauerkraut, and spaetzel while I enjoyed a mixed green salad with turkey cutlet. I looked for a grocery store after dinner but everything was closed so I bought milk and wine from the restaurant.

Day 43 Wednesday

Bolzano is lovely. I already know that I want to spend much more time in this area. We enjoyed lounging around in the morning. Wandered around town.

Day 44 Thursday Bolzano

Went to see the Ice Man museum today. Had lunch at a restaurant on the main square. Charged three times for the meal because the waiter was having problems with the new system. Language was a barrier. Need to go back tomorrow to get it fixed.

Day 45 Friday Verona

Stopped by the restaurant to fix the triple charge for the meal. The waiter was unable to understand the problem and insisted that we had not been overcharged. Finally, the manager came out and gave us a cash refund for the two erroneous charges. Took the train to Verona. Waited at a

Market in Bolzano, Italy

cute sidewalk café for our apartment to open. It turned out to be at the top of 4 flights of narrow stairs...no lift. It was an okay place, but wouldn't stay there again. Wandered around Verona in the evening. Took the Hop on Hop off bus tour. The arena in the main square looks interesting. Will go there tomorrow. Had dinner at a cute place overlooking the river.

Day 46. Saturday Verona

Paid the admission to visit the arena. It was the original coliseum upon which the Rome version was modeled. They were preparing for a concert, which was interesting. The back up band was doing a sound check. We stopped to listen for a while. Otherwise, the price of entry was kind of steep for what there was to see. We wandered around the historic area trying to find an ATM for quite some time. Couldn't ever find one. Had dinner in a cute restaurant.

Day 47 Sunday Cuggiono

We took the train through Milan and to a station that is nearby Cuggiono. Antonella picked us up. The apartment was simple, but very comfortable and right in the middle of town. The town was hosting the annual chocolate festival so we toured the booths and purchased some yummy chocolate. There are very few places to eat, but we luckily found a pizza place. Brought the pizza back to the apartment and ate on the small balcony overlooking the street and outwards to the main steeple. It's amazing that we were sitting looking at the same steeple that Brian's great grandparents saw each day before they immigrated to the US.

Day 48 Monday Cuggiono

We met Ernesto at the apartment at 9 am. He introduced us to many people. Showed us the museums, the vineyard in the park, and the street where the Garavalia's lived...Via Santa Maria! A group treated us to lunch at a local place in the other side of Cuggiono.

Day 49 Tuesday Turin

Antonella's brother took us to the train station. It was a fairly quick train ride to Turin. Our hotel apartment – Residence Sacchi – was within walking distance of the train station...almost directly across the street. Love the covered walkways throughout the historic area. Lots of small restaurants and shops along the walkways.

Day 50 Wednesday Turin

Took the hop on hop off bus around the city. There are a few different routes. Interesting drive through parks, past museums, through residential streets. The cathedral with the shroud of Turin is near the main hop on bus station. There was no entry into the church. Sat and enjoyed the peace for a bit. The palaces of the Savoy family surround the cathedral. Old roman ruins are also next to the church. Had lunch at an excellent old restaurant – Restaurante La Taverna dei Mercanti-- that was recommended by friends we met in Lucca.

Day 51 Thursday Turin

Had breakfast at home, then walked to the hop on hop off bus to take another line around the city. Then had lunch. Then took the third line around the city. Quiet evening and dinner at home.

Day 52 Friday Paris

We checked out of Residence Sacchi, walked down and across the street to Porta Nuovo station and took the train to Porta Susa. We had about an hour wait for our high speed train so we found a place to sit and got some pastries and water. The train was very nice. Eurail pass + reservation fee-- first class cabin. No free food or drinks, but there was a cafe car with good sandwiches. We brought them back to our seats and, overall, enjoyed the ride. The mountainous area outside of Turin is lovely. We'll need to see what small towns would make good day trips from Turin. It took 6 hours to get to Paris Gare de Lyon. Leaving the station, we joined long taxi line that moved fairly rapidly. All cabs have meters and the fare to Gare de L'Est was not bad. If we'd known the Okko hotel was actually in the train station, we probably would have taken the train instead of a taxi. At any rate, the fare was 17 euros and we rounded up to 20. He dropped us at a lift on the side-walk that said Okko Hotel but we didn't get a response to the intercom. A couple of nice gentlemen at the bar across the street directed us to walk down the train station stairs and find the hotel on the lower level. They were very helpful.

The hotel was new, opened in July. Quite modern...a large 'club' area with couches, tables, chairs, etc for community dining and relaxing. Our room was small, but efficient, quiet, and clean. The bed was comfy.

We explored the Gare L'Est station. Found the metro on the lower level. Went to the metro assistance counter to buy tickets. Bought 6 (about $12) to get started using the metro. You need one ticket per person per ride. Insert it into the ticket reader to open the gate. Pick it up from the top of the reader. Hold onto the ticket to be able to exit the metro at the other end. You have to insert the ticket into the reader at that end to open the exit gates. Similar to the London Oyster cards that have to be scanned at entry and exit from the tube.

Had dinner at the free hotel evening spread...6:30-9:00 and includes a free glass of wine each. Additional glass of wine is 5 euros.

Day 53 Saturday

We woke up early to leave the hotel by 6:30 to take line 4 on the metro to our meeting point for the Loire Valley tour. It turned out to be a big full bus. Unfortunately, the bus had no toilets and we didn't stop until 9:30. That was a miserably long time to wait for a bathroom break. Remember that next time when booking all day bus excursions. The Loire Valley was beautiful. We enjoyed seeing three different Châteaus. Had lunch at one which was a family run vineyard. Lunch served by the Count and his staff. We got back to Paris at 8 and then took the metro back to our hotel. Long day.

Day 54 Sunday

Brian ate the free hotel breakfast and I had cafe latte from the wonderful coffee machine. The breakfast spread was fairly extensive with hard boiled eggs, cheese, meats, rolls, pastries, cereals, fruit, etc.

We walked through the train station to try to find the ticket office for the hop on hop off boat. The tourist info booth gave us a brochure and told us to take the metro to the line 4 to the St Michel stop. From there, we found the Notre Dame stop for the Batobus. On the way, we took lots of pictures of Notre Dame. The building is under construction to fix the fire damage. Lots of fencing around the building and scaffolding around the burned area. The Batobus, fortunately, wasn't crowded at all. I enjoyed seeing all the amazing buildings lining the Seine and Bri stood on the back deck taking tons of pictures. We got off at the Musee d'Orsay stop and wandered along the upper riverwalk. Eventually, we came to the St Michel metro stop area. Before taking the metro back, we stopped for lunch. The food and service were okay. Next time, we need to research where we want to eat and be more purposeful about finding a quaint spot. We made dinner out of the free extensive hors d'oerves and wine at the hotel.

To prepare for the next day's journey, we took the metro to Gare du Nord, found the Eurostar gate, and bought more metro tickets to save time in the morning.

Day 55 Monday

We left the Okko hotel around 8. Walked through Gare L'Est to the metro. Went one stop to Gare du Nord. Went up to the Eurostar, checked in and then processed through French and U.K. customs. We were assigned to the A lounge area. Our train was scheduled for 10:31, but we arrived fairly early. Made a mistake and left with the crowd when the next boarding

224

happened. Turned out there was a 9:04 train. Luckily, no one else was assigned the seats we sat in and no one checked to see if we were on the
correct train. The seats were comfy and breakfast was nice...roll, croissant,
yogurt, juice, water, coffee/tea. We arrived in London around 10:30 with
the time change. The strategy to get to Windsor was a little tricky. We
stopped in the tourist information office in the St Pancras station. Luckily,
we already had our Oyster Passes and our Eurail passes so no need to buy
tickets. She gave us a map of the tube...take the Victoria line and get off at
Oxford Circus. Switch to the brown line to Waterloo Station. At Waterloo,
catch the train to Windsor Eton Riverside. A very nice man helped direct us
to make the tube connection to get to Waterloo Station with no problems.

The Crown and Cushion inn was about a 5 minute walk from the station,
just over the bridge in Eton. It was quite old and charming. The innkeeper
said it had been an inn and pub since the 1730s. The structure definitely
looked like it. Very charming, but totally wonky levels in the flooring. Our
room was so pitched that we kept sliding down the bed at night. It was

a teensy room but had a good size
bathroom, large enough to store our
open luggage in the bathroom. No air
conditioning, but it wasn't necessary.
The weather was chilly and rainy, just
what you might expect in London.
The best thing was the price, $79 per
night with free full breakfast. We ate
lunch and dinner in the pub. Excellent food. We wandered through
Eton during the afternoon. Light driz-
zle until the end of our walk when it
started raining more earnestly.

**Windsor Castle,
Windsor, England**

Day 56 Tuesday

Brian ate the free breakfast at the inn and I tried to stave off eating to
reduce my eating window for the day. We wandered through Windsor by
the castle to the long walk. We only walked about ¼ of the way. No toilets
in the Great Park as far as we could tell. Stopped in Mark & Spence back in
town. Nice toilets on the upper floor, right next to the stairs.

It was an overcast, somewhat chilly day. Walking was not as enjoyable as on a sunny day. We decided to take a river boat cruise...45 minutes, 19 pounds. It was narrated and interesting to see the homes and lands near the town...horse tracks, swan sanctuary, Eton College in the distance.

Lunch was at a lovely riverside restaurant. After, we went back to the inn. We went out again later for a bit more walking. Dinner at the inn.

Day 57 Wednesday

We left the Crown and Cushion at 7:45 to take the 8:21 train from Riverside station to Gatwick via Clapham Junction. We arrived at Gatwick with no problems. Walked through the train station to the airport shuttle and took it to the North terminal. Since we were not checking any bags, we used the self service kiosk with a little help from the Virgin Atlantic rep... scanning passport and printing boarding card. Luckily, we booked priority boarding so we walked through the priority security line. They're very efficient in dividing people into different spaces on the conveyer belt so 5 people are putting all their things in bins at one time. After security, we walked through a curvy, very long duty free shopping area. We went upstairs in the food court and found a Lebanese restaurant for breakfast. It was quite good. I had scrambled eggs on toast and they sprinkled pomegranate seeds on top. Really tasty. Brian had pancakes with honey and banana.

After breakfast, we waited in the large open lounge area. Gatwick doesn't assign gates until boarding time so all flights wait together. We boarded at 12:05 for our 1:00 flight. I got pulled aside for additional screening. We had premium economy seats with adequate leg room and excellent food. In Orlando, we also had extra security screening through customs. Apparently, it's a problem if you ever visited a farm while traveling. After customs, we called Penny, our shuttle, to pick us up. Made it home around 8 pm.

CHAPTER 14:
TRAVEL DOCUMENTS FOR US TOURISTS

Chapter 14: Travel Documents for US Tourists

- Passports
- Short-stay visas
- European Travel Information and Authorisation System (ETIAS) tourist visa waivers

Passports

US citizens must have a valid US passport to travel in Europe. Before making any travel plans, check the expiration date of your passport. A number of countries require that you have at least 6 months remaining on your passport prior to exiting their country. If you won't have at least 6 months validity upon your planned exit, apply for a new passport immediately (https://www.usa.gov/passport). It's possible that you won't experience any problems with an imminent expiration date, but it's not worth taking a chance. Better safe than sorry.

US passport application process

Find out how to get a new passport or renew your existing passport by visiting the US passport website for instructions (https://www.usa.gov/passport). Once you submit an application, passport renewal typically takes 10-12 weeks; however, since the pandemic, longer wait times of up to 18 weeks have been reported. An expedited process usually takes 4-6 weeks, but you must pay a higher processing fee. Options are available for emergency processing, as well, if you find that you must travel immediately. Read the instructions on the US government passport website to find which passport application option suits your situation.

If you plan to travel soon, check your passport now to decide if you need to renew. We renewed our passports during the summer of 2020 at the height of the coronavirus pandemic. The regional passport processing center had limited operations, and we were very concerned that our passports would not be returned before our planned departure that July, even though we mailed our paperwork 3 months in advance.

You can check the passport processing website to see the progress of your application. When renewing our passports, the site reported that our applications were not yet "in process" six weeks after we submitted the applications. Luckily, a friend told us to ask our local congressperson for help. We looked up the US representative office nearest our home and called. A staff member in the office is assigned to assist constituents with passports as part of his job responsibilities. He tracked down our passport renewal applications within a couple of days and made sure that our passports were processed in time for our trip. Consider contacting your US representative's office if you experience any issues or delay in your passport renewal.

The directions on the US government passport website are easy to follow. You don't need to pay a service to help you obtain a passport. Just follow the instructions and call the customer service number if you need assistance.

Currently, there is no way to submit your application online. Print the application and then use black ink to fill in the form. In addition to the application, you will need several passport photos. Although phone apps are available to help you create your own passport photos, we found it easier to use a local passport photo service. The nearest one to us was in a CVS store. Passport photos were available with walk-in service, no appointment, no wait. The store clerk printed the photos in the correct size in the appropriate format. We left with photos in hand.

Passport photo format is very important. Make sure to say that you need the photos for a US passport. We had extra copies printed, just in case we decide to apply for a long-stay visa in another country. Long-stay visas might require you to use the same photo as on your passport. Use Google or a similar search engine to find a passport photo store near you.

First-time passport applicants

The list of requirements for first-time passport applicants is slightly different than renewals. A first-time applicant must submit

- the passport application
- an original proof of citizenship document (e.g. birth certificate, naturalization papers)
- copy of the front and back of the proof of citizenship document
- passport photos

- copy of front and back of government issued photo ID (e.g. driver license)
- passport processing fee – personal check, money order, or exact amount of cash.

If you are applying for a passport for the first time, you will need to apply in-person at a Passport Acceptance Facility. Use the Internet to find the nearest facility. Go to this website https://iafdb.travel.state.gov/ and type in your zip code to find the nearest center.

Passport renewals

For renewals, you can usually submit the application through the mail. However, check the instructions on the US government website. You may need to submit your application in-person if your old passport was

- issued more than 15 years ago;
- you were less than 16 when the passport was issued; or
- your old passport was damaged, lost, or stolen.

If you are mailing your application, we recommend that you use a mailing service (e.g. FedEx) that will provide a tracking number so that you know when your application reaches the processing center. The appropriate processing center for your region can be found at (https://www.usa.gov/passport). Mail the following items to the appropriate processing center for your region of the US:

- Completed application
- Most recent passport
- Passport photos (attached to the application correctly)
- Marriage license or other evidence of a name change, if applicable
- Payment of passport fees (check or money order)

Checking the status of your passport application

After 14 days, you may check the status of your application online https://passportstatus.state.gov/ or by calling 1-877-487-2778 to speak to customer service. Provide your last name, date of birth, and the last four digits of your social security number. The status check system will tell you NOT FOUND, IN PROCESS, APPROVED, or MAILED.

Receiving your passports

After your new passports have been mailed to you, the passport processing center will return your old passport in a separate mailing (if applicable). Keep in mind that your new passport will not have the same passport number as your old passport. This is important to know if you are booking travel (e.g. Eurail passes) that requires a passport number. Last year, we booked our Eurail passes with our expiring passports. When our passports arrived, we realized that the new passport numbers did not correspond to the passport numbers on our rail passes. Worried about our mistake, we consulted the ticket agent at our first train stop in Europe. We showed both our old and new passports to the ticket agent and explained our mistake. The agent kindly granted us leeway given the current pandemic and difficult travel environment. It worked out for us, but we always prefer to avoid that type of stress when traveling. Wait to book travel, such as rail passes, until you have your new passports with the new number.

Note: Some circumstances may restrict one's ability to obtain or renew a US passport...excessive back taxes owed to IRS, unpaid child support, or felony drug convictions. Check the government website or call the passport customer service if you believe you may be restricted in some way.

Traveling with your passport

Prior to leaving on your trip, make a few photocopies of your passport. Leave a copy with your emergency contact person in the US. Pack a copy in your luggage, and as an extra precaution, take a picture and store it in your phone.

Be aware that the local police in Europe may ask to see your passport at any time. For example, Brian was waiting for me at the train station in Bolzano, Italy, and two police officers asked him for his passport. They asked him several questions about what he was doing and where he was going. Be aware that this could happen at any time. Be prepared to show your passport and your travel documents, such as train tickets and hotel reservations. If you entered the country as a tourist (as opposed to on a work visa or other long-stay visa), then always say that you are a tourist.

You will need to show your passport at many points in your travel process. Be sure to keep your passport in a safe and handy place. When you arrive at the airport, you will need to scan it at the boarding pass kiosk or show it to the ticket agent when you check-in for your flight. You will likely discover that you aren't able to check-in online prior to going to the airport. This is because the airline must document that they have checked your passport. Check-in will be in-person at an airport kiosk or ticket counter where your passport will be scanned into the travel system.

Your passport will be checked again when you clear airport security and at the departure gate when you board the flight....again at passport control at your destination airport...and again when you check-in to your hotel. Be aware that your host (e.g. front desk clerk or apartment host) will make a copy of your passport as required by law. Most European countries require hosts to register guests with the local police and to provide a copy of the guest's passport. Lastly, most travel passes require you to present your passport with the pass (e.g. Eurail pass) when you are using it. I have a passport carry case that I wear around my neck and under my top layer of clothing. Brian has travel pants with zipper pockets for easy access and security from pickpockets. Both options are also handy for carrying a bit of cash and your credit cards.

How do countries keep track of who's coming and going: E-Passports

All United States passports have been e-passports since 2007. This means a microchip (RFID chip: radio frequency identification) is embedded inside the cover that holds a copy of the personal contact information found on the photo page of your passport, including the photo. If you enter through an ePassport gate scanner, it will read the information contained in the chip while a camera takes a picture of the traveler. An officer at a control station behind these gates then checks to see if the newly taken photo matches the one on your passport (facial recognition). Some countries no longer stamp passports. It's up to the traveler to keep a record of when he/she entered the country (e.g. a flight receipt). Beginning in 2022, the Schengen area will begin using a new EES (Entry/Exit System) to better track movement across its borders and keep track of tourist stays in the area.

For any other questions about US passports, the following site is helpful https://travel.state.gov/content/travel/en/passports.html

Short-stay Visas

All countries have stay restrictions for tourists, and the rules vary for travelers depending upon citizenship. Know the stay restrictions for US citizens for the country you are visiting to avoid deportation or other problems (see Table 1).

Tourist Visas in Europe prior to 2022

Most European countries allow US citizens to visit the country for a limited period of time as a tourist without any formal documents. This type of "visa" is called a "tourist visa." As a US citizen, you don't need to take any action to be granted a tourist visa in Europe...no application, no paperwork. When passport control asks you why you are entering their country, simply tell them that you are a tourist.

At the time of this writing, 26 European countries are members of the Schengen area. The short-stay tourist visa is automatic and allows a US citizen to stay 90 out of 180 days in the Schengen area, moving across country borders freely. As long as you haven't already used up your entitlement in the last 90 days, US citizens aren't required to do anything in advance to enjoy a short-stay visa – no stickers, no letters, no forms...just enter a Schengen country and get your passport stamped (or ePassport scanned).

The tourist visa stay restriction is a rolling 90-day period so calculate your stay by counting backward from your planned exit date. If you plan to stay in the Schengen area longer than three months, you need to apply for a visa prior to leaving the US on your trip. This is very important, in some cases you may be asked to return to your home country to re-apply. Contact the embassy of the country where you plan to spend the majority of your time to apply for a long-stay visa for the Schengen area.

Be aware that the length of tourist visas vary across Europe. In the Schengen area, US citizens may stay 90 out of 180 days. In the United Kingdom (England, Wales, Scotland, Northern Ireland), US citizens may stay for 6 months. See Table 1 for tourist-visa stay restrictions for each European country for US citizens.

Some people mistakenly believe that you can step outside of a country for a day or two and then restart the tourist visa clock when you reenter. NOT TRUE. Before you travel, look up the tourist visa rules for the countries that you intend to visit. Most have a rule that you can stay (x) number of days out of (y) period. For example, in the UK, US tourists may stay 6 months out of a year.

Table 1: Stay restrictions for US tourist visas for all European countries, March 2021.

Schengen area countries 90 out of last 180 days	Non-Schengen countries Tourism visa varies for each country	
Austria (EU)	Albania	North Macedonia
Belgium (EU)	Up to one year	Up to 90 days within a 6
Czechia (EU)		month period
Denmark (EU)		
Estonia (EU)	Andorra	Moldova
Finland (EU)	Periods up to 3 months	Up to 90 days within a 6
France (EU)		month period
Germany (EU)		
Greece (EU)	Armenia	Monaco
Hungary (EU)	180 days per year	Up to 90 days within a 6
Iceland		month period
Italy (EU)		
Latvia (EU)	Azerbaijan	Montenegro
Lithuania (EU)	Up to 30 days	Up to 90 days
Luxembourg (EU)		
Malta (EU)	Belarus	Romania (EU)
Netherlands (EU)	No more than 90 days	(seeking to join Schen-
Norway	total in a calendar year	gen area)
Poland (EU)		Up to 90 days within a
Portugal (EU)		180 day period
Slovakia (EU)		
Slovenia (EU)	Bosnia & Herzegovina	Russia
Spain (EU)	Up to 90 days within a	Up to 180 days in a row
Sweden (EU)	period of 6 months	
Switzerland		
	Bulgaria (EU) (seeking to	San Marino
Vatican City treated as	join Schengen area)	Up to 90 of the last 180
part of the Schengen	Up to 90 days within 6	days
Area for tourist visas	months	
	Croatia (EU) (seeking to	
	join Schengen area)	
	Up to 90 days	

Schengen area countries 90 out of last 180 days	Non-Schengen countries Tourism visa varies for each country	
	Croatia (EU) (seeking to join Schengen area) Up to 90 days	Serbia Up to 90 days within a 180 day period
	Cyprus (EU) (seeking to join Schengen area) Up to 90 days	Turkey Up to 90 days
	Georgia Up to 365 days	Ukraine Up to 90 days
	Ireland (EU) Up to 90 days	The United Kingdom (EU) Up to 6 months in a year per stay
	Kosovo Up to 90 days within 6 months	

Note: Online calculators can help you determine how long you can stay in the Schengen area. See this website for an easy-to-use calculator. https://ec.europa.eu/assets/home/visa-calculator/calculator.htm?lang=en

Always consult the Travel.State.Gov website or the destination country government website for specific rules for your destination countries prior to travel.

Penalty for overstaying a visa

When moving from country to country in the Schengen, the tourist visa clock does not reset. Visits in Schengen countries accumulate as if in a single country. If you overstay the tourist visa period in the Schengen area or any country, you may be deported. Even if you are not physically removed from the country, your passport may be stamped with "deported" as you exit the country. You may be levied a very expensive fine. Lastly, you may be banned from reentering the country or the entire Schengen area for a period of time or even forever. Don't overstay your visa.

ETIAS visa waiver (to go into effect in 2022)

European countries are implementing a new electronic visa waiver system to increase security, combat terrorism, and reduce threats to national or global security. To that end, US tourists (and other foreign nationals) will need to apply to the European Travel Information and Authorisation System (ETIAS) beginning in the latter part of 2022. A successful applicant will be granted an ETIAS visa waiver with a 3-year validity. See the website for more information: https://etias.com/etias-requirements.

According to the website, US tourists must provide the following information through the ETIAS visa waiver application:

1. Surname (family name), first name(s), surname at birth, usual name(s); date of birth, place of birth, country of birth, sex, current nationality, first names of the parents of the applicant; home address;

2. Passport and / or Travel document information;

3. If applicable, information on any other nationalities or citizenships;

4. Address of permanent residence;

5. Email address and telephone number;

6. Member State of intended first entry;

7. Education and / or current occupation information;

8. ETIAS background and eligibility questions. Such questions will pertain to any medical conditions or other infectious or contagious parasitic diseases; criminal history involving serious damage to property, to another person or entity; history of distributing illegal drugs; previous travel to war-zone countries as well as any previous immigration or travel history which resulted in the applicant being deported or rejected entry into an EU member country;

9. If the applicant is a minor, the identity of the person responsible for

the minor;

0. If the application is submitted by a person different of the applicant, the identity of the person and company that he or she represents (if applicable).

1. For family members to EU citizens/third country nationals benefitting from free movement without residence cards: their status as family member; the identity details of the family member with whom the applicant has ties; their family ties.

US travelers must also answer some basic security questions with the ETIAS visa waiver application, such as:

• Criminal history
• Employment history
• Drug use
• Human trafficking
• Prior travel to conflict areas
• Past European travel information

After answering all of the required security questions on the ETIAS form, US tourists must pay the required ETIAS fee (7 euros, as of March 2021) using either a valid credit or debit card to make the payment. The applicant will then receive confirmation for the ETIAS visa waiver through email. The ETIAS visa waiver permits travel to Europe. Note that ETIAS is an electronic system linked to the traveler's passport. There is no need to apply before every trip. Again, the ETIAS visa waiver permits travel during its 3-year validity.

CHAPTER 15:
LONGER-TERM LIVING IN EUROPE

Chapter 15:
Longer-term living in Europe

- How to extend your stay without getting a visa
- How to get a visa and temporary residency permit
- How to apply for citizenship
- Important financial considerations
  - Banking issues for US citizens who reside in Europe
  - What to do about US investments while living in Europe
  - Income taxes while residing in Europe

First, you may wonder if there are any restrictions on absence from the US. There is no time limit if you are a US citizen (native or naturalized). For permanent residents or conditional permanent residents, check with the state department, but the length of absence is usually 6 months.

If you intend to be gone for more than 6 months, check with a tax accountant and your financial advisor to make sure that you are in compliance with US regulatory rules for taxation and investment. If you're re-

View from Marjan Hill, Split, Croatia

tired, you likely do not intend to earn money from activities during your travels. If you are blogging or doing other internet-based work, be sure to verify that you are not creating any tax liabilities in another country if you're staying beyond the usual tourist limits.

Also, for longer-term stays in Europe, be sure to check with your investment broker as to rules for investing in the US stock market. Rules for investing are different if you are not a resident of the United States (i.e. you have obtained a visa and a residency permit in another country). In exploring options for long-term stay in Italy, we learned that we would need to identify an Attorney-in-Fact (AIF) to approve investment transactions if we became official residents of Italy. However, residency should not be a problem if you are maintaining your primary residence in the US, and you do not seek a residency permit in another country.

How to extend your stay in Europe without getting a visa

A number of options are available to US citizens who wish to stay in Europe for long periods of time.

Option 1: Suppose you would like to remain in Europe for a year, but don't want to go through the hassle of applying for a visa at an embassy consulate in the US prior to travel. The US enjoys visa waivers with European countries, so you don't need to apply for a visa as long as you limit the number of days within each country/region to those allowed for US tourists (see Table 1). It's actually easy for a US citizen to stay in Europe for an extended period of time if you're willing to move around among a number of countries.

Blue Mosque, Istanbul, Turkey

In general, non-Schengen countries allow stays anywhere from 60 to 365 days. Suppose you fly from the US to London (UK). You are allowed to stay in the UK up to 6 months in a 1-year period. Within the UK British Isles, you can enjoy England, Scotland, Wales, and Northern Ireland. From the UK, take the Eurostar (English Channel train) to a western European country (the Netherlands, France, Belgium, etc.) in the Schengen area. Spend the next 90 days in the Schengen area, and then move on to a non-Schengen country for another 90 days (e.g. Croatia, Serbia, Montenegro, Albania, Ireland). This travel route allows an entire year in Europe without a long-stay visa.

You could actually stay indefinitely by visiting countries/regions that are independent of one another with regard to tourist visas. One year, we spent considerable time in Serbia and then Croatia before traveling to Schengen countries. Serbia and Croatia both have tourist visa rules that are independent of any other countries. We could have stayed in each of those European countries for the maximum tourist stay-- 90 days in Serbia and then another 90 days in Croatia. We could then have also stayed in the Schengen area for an additional 90 days. Leaving the Schengen, we visited England where we could have stayed for 6 months. See Table 1 for a complete list of tourist stay restrictions in European countries.

Option 2: Take advantage of a bilateral agreement (see the etiasvisa.com website for more details). US citizens may stay longer than the 90/180 day limit through a bilateral visa-waiver reciprocal agreement between the United States and several European nations. There are restrictions, however, and these agreements are subject to change. As of March 2021, the following European countries allow stays beyond the 90/180 day rule for US tourists:

Belgium (3 months)
Denmark (3 months)
Italy (3 months)
Hungary (90 days)
Portugal (60 days)
Spain (90 days)
France (90 days)
Latvia (90 days in half a year)
The Netherlands (90 days)

The rules are different for each of these countries regarding how to obtain and use an extension. In some countries, you'll need to exit the Schengen area or the country, and, then, re-enter the country in which you are extending your stay. Check the country's government website to find the rules for the country of interest.

In order to request a bilateral visa waiver extension, the US traveler must ask for permission to stay at some point in time prior to the expiration of the initial 90-day tourist visa. Keep in mind that the country may deny the request, so ask before making travel commitments that extend beyond the initial 90 day tourist short-stay visa.

he restrictions for US passport holders who take advantage of one of these visa waiver bilateral agreements are as follows:

The US traveler must remain in that specific country for the entire extension (i.e. may not leave that country).
The traveler must exit the Schengen Area from that EU nation.
On departure, it is necessary to fly directly to a third country outside of the EU or transit in a non-Schengen airport.

Here's an example: A US tourist with an ordinary US passport travels through Schengen countries for 90 days. The tourist wants to remain in Italy for an additional 90 days. US tourists may stay in Italy for a 90-day extension regardless of time spent in other Schengen countries prior to the extension. If the tourist wants to remain in a different bilateral agreement country, then he/she will need to make that the final stop in the initial 90-day period AND make the request for an extension in that country. If staying in Italy, the US traveler might leave from Milan with a flight to Heathrow at the end of the extension, thus flying to a third country, non-EU airport.

The Acropolis of Athens, Greece

It's up to the traveler to document compliance with extension rules. Here are some suggestions to document that you stayed in your designated country during your extension:

- Enter the country by plane, bus or train and retain the ticket stub (make sure it indicates the date)
- Keep hard copies of your receipts for groceries, meals, tourist attractions
- Save a copy of your lodging rental agreement or hotel receipts

Be aware that relying on staying with the bilateral visa waiver could be a risky strategy as officials may be unfamiliar with the option. We consulted the Italian Embassy Consulate in Miami to confirm that we could use this strategy and were told that US tourists could only stay 90 out of 180 days in Italy. In addition, we read a blogger's account of trying to use the agreement in France with the same lack of success. See etiasvisa.com for more information.

How to get a visa and temporary residency permit

First, here's a quick distinction between long-stay visas and residency permits.

- Visas are obtained prior to leaving the United States. Border control checks your visa when you enter a new country to make sure you are allowed in that country. The visa has a validity period and a specific duration.
- A residence permit is different. The permit provides permission to stay in the country for longer than the tourist visa entitlement (e.g. 90 out of 180 days) and is usually obtained once you're already in the country
- You will need both a long-stay visa and residency permit to stay in the country for an extended period of time.
- A US citizen will need to apply for a long-stay visa before departing for Europe while still in the United States. This is very important. You cannot apply for a long-stay visa from the country in which you wish to stay. You must apply in the United States.

Some of the terminology related to visas and permits might be a bit confusing. There are basically 4 types of visa categories: A, B, C, and D.

"A" and "B" are transit visas that allow the holder to travel in transit to another destination. US citizens are generally allowed to transit through and visit the Schengen Area and other European countries without a visa so you shouldn't have to worry about these two types.

"C" is a short-term visa that allows the holder to reside in the Schengen Area or other European countries for no more than the stay restrictions for tourists (see Table 1). This visa can be a Single-entry, Double-entry, or Multiple-entry visa. See the Schengen website or the government website of your destination country for more information on the specifics of each type of entry visa. US citizens do not usually need to do anything to obtain this visa other than enter the European country through passport control and receive a passport stamp. Note that the visa-free entitlement is for US citizens only. Research the rules if you are a green card holder or other resident of the US.

The "D" is a long-stay visa (also called a National Visa). This visa can be a Single-entry, Double-entry, or Multiple-entry. See the Schengen website or the government website for your destination country for more information on the specifics of each type of entry visa. Note that the multiple-entry visa can be for 1, 3, or 5 years.

La Sagrada Familia, Barcelona, Spain

A national visa (type D) for any of the Schengen countries automatically allows you to travel throughout the Schengen during the visa validity period. The holder is allowed to study, work, or live (per the specific type of visa) in a Schengen country for longer than 90 days. You must apply for the visa while in the US prior to departing for Europe. The national visa is issued in the US by consular authorities for the specific Schengen country. To obtain a multi-entry national visa, you must meet certain criteria, such as:

- International student participating in a program of one year or less duration.
- International student starting a full course of studies in one of the Schengen countries. The visa is issued for a period of one year with the possibility of extending it.
- Pedagogical work at a higher institution or research center in any of the Schengen countries, for the person and close family members.
- A professional traveling in any of the Schengen countries due to his/her expertise be it a sportsman, an artist or any other professional of its kind with the purpose of sharing its expertise.

- Emergency cases, such as a medical condition that prevents the individual from leaving the Schengen Area as originally required.

The criteria are similar for other European countries that are not in the Schengen area. Once you have identified the specific country you wish to visit, carefully read the government website to ensure that you comply with the visa guidelines. As a retiree, you may wish to be an "international student" enrolled in a language or cultural education program. If so, check to ensure that the college or university is recognized as an allowable institution for receiving a long-stay visa.

You have a number of long-term visa options for living in Europe: a student, work, retirement, investment, business/entrepreneur (for small- and medium-sized businesses), self-employment, digital nomad, spousal/partner, and citizenship via descent, to name a few. Countries vary as to how much cash you must have in the bank or in investments to qualify for the retiree (elective) visa. Some countries allow you to "invest" in the country to basically buy residency and ultimately citizenship. All countries require that you have sufficient means to support yourself, documentation of adequate health insurance, and a place to stay while in Europe.

A long-stay visa is necessary for US citizens who wish to stay for more than 90 days in Europe with a couple of exceptions that are described in the next section (see options 1 or 2 for extended stay). A US citizen may also need to apply for a visa if staying in the Schengen area for purposes other than those permitted with an ETIAS visa waiver. Allowable travel reasons by ETIAS include

- Tourism
- Business
- Medical Treatment
- Transit

To work requires a work visa and to study requires a study visa. Most European countries also allow retirees to apply for a long-stay visa. Remember, visas can be obtained from the destination country embassy located in the United States. You will need to consult the country embassy website to find out the jurisdiction for your US home address.

Difference between Visa Validity and Duration of Stay

When you apply for a visa, the embassy appoints the number of days you are permitted to stay in any of the Schengen countries, as well as the first date you are permitted to enter the Schengen area and the last day that you are permitted to remain. There is a difference between visa validity and duration of stay.

Duration of Stay – maximum number of days you are permitted to remain in the Schengen area. The first day you enter the Schengen is counted as "Day 1" and the day you leave is counted as the last day.

Visa Validity – dates (example: January 1 to January 30) for which you can use your visa to enter and stay in the Schengen Area.

Bosphorus Bridge connecting Europe and Asia, Istanbul, Turkey

Example: Suppose you have a duration of stay for your visa of 30 days and the validity of your visa is January 1 to January 30. If you enter the Schengen on January 15, you must still leave by January 30 in order to comply with the validity period, even though you have not used all of the days in your allowable duration of stay.

How to get a visa

Overview of process for obtaining visas for longer stays

- Secure a place to reside in your designated country for the entire stay of your visa request...usually at least 1 year
- Gather all relevant documents for the type of visa you have selected, complete the visa application, and submit all of the paperwork to the correct embassy consulate in the US
- Attend an interview at the embassy consulate in the US
- Wait for your visa to arrive in the mail
- Travel to the European country of your visa

Next: Apply for a temporary residency permit within the designated time period (e.g. for Italy, you must apply within 8 days of entering the country)

Decide on the specific country for your visa application.	Many Schengen countries use a common visa application. Italy and France have their own applications. Check the government website for your destination country for a copy of the correct visa application.
Determine which visa type you need. Common options are	<ul><li>Tourism</li><li>Visa for visiting family and friends</li><li>Work visa</li><li>Business or entrepreneur visa</li><li>Visa for culture and sport activities</li><li>Study visa</li><li>Retiree (e.g., elective, passive income) visa</li><li>Visa for medical reasons</li></ul>
Find a place to stay and obtain documentation for at least 1 year from your date of entry to the country	<ul><li>Property lease</li><li>Property purchase</li><li>Staying with a friend or family member</li><li>Accommodations provided by work or school</li></ul>
Find out where you need to apply in the United States.	<ul><li>The destination country's embassy</li><li>A consulate of the destination country's embassy</li><li>A visa center to which the embassy of your destination country has outsourced visa processing</li><li>The embassy/consulate of another Schengen country to which the embassy of your destination country has outsourced visa submission</li></ul>

Find the suitable time to apply	It could be as long as 8 months and up until 15 days prior to travel. Recommended time is at least 3 weeks prior to travel. You must apply at least 15 days in advance to allow sufficient time for processing.
Book an appointment at the visa processing place (e.g. embassy, consulate)	
Complete the appropriate long-stay visa application form. Note that Italy and France have their own forms. The website schengenvisainfo.com has a link to the visa application forms for other Schengen countries.	
On the day of your appointment,	a) show up on time at the facility where you will be interviewed b) meet with a visa consular and submit your collected documents and application c) answer all questions about your whereabouts, the intended trip and other travel details in a consistent manner with your visa application. d) Typical interview questions • Which countries are you planning to visit? • Do you have any family members or friends living in Europe? • What is the purpose of your visit?

Gathering the paperwork for your visa application

The visa application is submitted to and the interview takes place in-person in the United States at the destination country's embassy consulate. You must use the embassy consulate that is designated for your jurisdiction. For example, we live in Florida and the embassy consulate for Italy is in Miami. We live in the jurisdiction of the Miami embassy; therefore, we must apply for a visa at the Italian embassy consulate in Miami. Keep in mind that jurisdictions may span many states. For example, my sister lives in South Carolina, and her home address also falls within the Miami jurisdiction for Italy. Be sure to check the destination country's government website for the jurisdiction for your US home address.

In general, required documents include

A completed application form for a Schengen long-stay visa or national visa for your destination country
Copies of any previously issued Schengen visas
A valid US passport containing at least 2 blank pages and with an adequate remaining validity
Any accommodation bookings the traveler has made for their stay
Round trip flight tickets, or tickets to an onward destination
Proof of sufficient financial means to cover the stay in Europe
Travel insurance which covers medical care in the Schengen Area
A recent, passport-sized, photograph of the traveler, taken against a white background
A cover letter explaining why you are requesting a visa

If you are applying for a study visa, then you'll also need the official certificate from the university/college/school program.

If you're moving to France from the US, you'll need to apply for a visa de long séjour, which enables you to stay for up to a year without a residence permit. According to Expatica, this requires you to be any of the following:

Employed on a year-long contract, or a temporary worker with a contract between three months and a year

A scientific researcher
A student or intern
Married to a French citizen
The spouse of a foreign national living legally in France

How to get a residence permit

You will need a residency permit if you are staying in a country or the Schengen area more than the allowed tourist stay limit. To be eligible, you will first need a long-stay visa as described above. Then, usually, you apply for a permit in the city or region where you are staying. You'll need to fill out an application and submit it to the proper authorities. Each country varies with regard to the exact process. For example, in Italy, you'll need to pick up a "kit" at the post-office and complete the required paperwork within 8 days of arriving in Italy. In some countries, the permit involves confirmation of your accommodations. You will likely receive a visit to your "home" (the residence that you have listed in your permit application) from the local police to verify that you are residing in that location. Initial residency permits are "temporary" residency permits. After 5 years, you may apply for a long-term residency permit.

Once you have your visa and have established residency in a European country, you are free to visit other countries at will. You can stay as long as you like, as long as you comply with the conditions of your visa and residency permit. It's easier to obtain visas and residency permits in some countries. Portugal and Spain are often cited as good examples of countries amenable to longer visits for US citizens. A good strategy might be to find a country with relatively easy entry requirements and processes, establish temporary residency in that country, and then travel wherever you'd like in Europe for as long as you'd like.

Summary of Process for obtaining your long-stay visa and temporary residency permit

An overview of the steps for obtaining a visa and residency permit are outlined below. If you would like more information about a specific type of visa and residency permit, read the full description and examples from

Brussels, Belgium

real-life bloggers who have made the move to Europe as students or retirees.

Obtaining a visa and residency permit

While you're in the US
Decide which type of long-stay visa you need (study, work, retiree, investment, digital nomad, entrepreneur, etc.). Consult the government website for your destination country to see the options that are available.

Secure a rental contract for an accommodation for the length of your entire visa or buy a property

Students may stay in a holiday let, student dormitory, as a guest of a person already living in Italy

A retiree visa usually requires a specific type of rental contract. Consult the government website of your destination country. For example, Italy requires that any rental property

After receiving a long-stay visa, obtain a temporary residency permit
1: Obtain your long-stay visa which includes evidence that you have accommodations for the period of your long-stay visa
2. Obtain a tax identification number, if required
3. Seek a residency permit (e.g. an Italian Permesso di Soggiorno)
4. The police or other officials will verify that you are living in the accommodations that you listed on your application.
5. Obtain an identification card (e.g. an Italian Carta d'Identita)

Typically, an advantage of obtaining residency in an EU country provides the option to travel among the other European countries freely. A number of residency permits are available.

...As a person of independent means
For retirees, the easiest way might be to apply for a residency as a person of independent means. Spain, Portugal, Austria, Cypress, and Ireland provide this path as an option for residency. The applicant must demonstrate an amount of annual passive income and a few other criteria, such as, a letter of good standing from home police office, full health insurance with coverage in Europe, and possibly a required level of education. In some cases, you may even work while you're in the country. See the government website for the relevant country for procedures on obtaining this visa.

...Through investment in the country
Many European countries offer a residency by investment option. Often the investment is 500,000 euros or higher. Depending on the country, it could be investment in real estate or a business. Countries with this option include Spain, Portugal, Bulgaria, Latvia, Italy, Malta, Greece, Cyprus,

...As an entrepreneur starting a business in the country
Related to the above two visas are start-up visas for entrepreneurs. Applicants must prove that they have the expertise to start and run the business, the appropriate funds to start the business, and sufficient resources on which to live.

...As a digital nomad
Estonia has a digital nomad visa. Applicants must prove location indepen-

dent income of at least 3500 euros per month. The visa is good for one year.

How to apply for long-term residency and citizenship

Brussels, Belgium

It's possible to live long-term in a European country by continuing to renew your temporary residency permit each year or each time it expires. After 5 years, you'll be able to apply for a long-term residency permit. For example, in Italy, after you have been a temporary resident for 5 years, you may apply to be a permanent resident which is a 5-year permit.

A long-term resident in the European Union is defined as a person who is not a citizen of an EU country but has resided legally and continuously within its territory for five years with a means of support (i.e. without recourse to the social assistance system of the host country) and fulfills some further requirements, as defined in Directive 2003/109/EC.[1] The status permits the holder some of the rights of free movement afforded to EU/EEA citizens in the participating countries.

The eligibility criteria for US citizens (and others) for a long-term residence permit are:

254

Residence in the EU country where you apply for at least 5 years. These 5 years would likely be met through temporary residency.

Sufficient financial means to support yourself and any dependents who may be residing with you in Europe.

Sufficient command of the official language of the country in which you are seeking an EU residence permit.

Basic knowledge of the legal and social system and the way of life in the country in which you are seeking a residence permit.

Sufficient living space for yourself and any dependents who may be residing with you.

ou may forego much of the paperwork if you are married to a citizen of he EU. Following are the rules for residing in the EU as a family member f an EU citizen.

Right of residence for more than three months

.. All Union citizens shall have the right of residence on the territory of nother Member State for a period of longer than three months if they:

a) are workers or self-employed persons in the host Member State; or

b) have sufficient resources for themselves and their family members not o become a burden on the social assistance system of the host Member State during their period of residence and have comprehensive sickness nsurance cover in the host Member State; or

c) are enrolled at a private or public establishment, accredited or financed by the host Member State on the basis of its legislation or administrative practice, for the principal purpose of following a course of study, including vocational training; and
— have comprehensive sickness insurance cover in the host Member State and assure the relevant national authority, by means of a declaration or by such equivalent means as they may choose, that they have sufficient resources for themselves and their family members not to become a burden on the social assistance system of the host Member State during their period of residence; or

(d) are family members accompanying or joining a Union citizen who satisfies the conditions referred to in points (a), (b) or (c).

2. The right of residence provided for in paragraph 1 shall extend to family members who are not nationals of a Member State, accompanying or joining the Union citizen in the host Member State, provided that such Union citizen satisfies the conditions referred to in paragraph 1(a), (b) or (c).

3. For the purposes of paragraph 1(a), a Union citizen who is no longer a worker or self-employed person shall retain the status of worker or self-employed person in the following circumstances:

(a) he/she is temporarily unable to work as the result of an illness or accident;

(b) he/she is in duly recorded involuntary unemployment after having been employed for more than one year and has registered as a job-seeker with the relevant employment office;

(c) he/she is in duly recorded involuntary unemployment after completing a fixed-term employment contract of less than a year or after having become involuntarily unemployed during the first twelve months and has registered as a job-seeker with the relevant employment office. In this case, the status of worker shall be retained for no less than six months;

(d) he/she embarks on vocational training. Unless he/she is involuntarily unemployed, the retention of the status of worker shall require the training to be related to the previous employment.

4. By way of derogation from paragraphs 1(d) and 2 above, only the spouse, the registered partner provided for in Article 2(2)(b) and dependent children shall have the right of residence as family members of a Union citizen meeting the conditions under 1(c) above. Article 3(2) shall apply to his/her dependent direct relatives in the ascending lines and those of his/her spouse or registered partner.

How to Apply for Citizenship

The ultimate way to stay in Europe is to become a citizen of one of the European countries. A number of European countries allow dual citizenship with the United States.

Belgium
Czech Republic
Cyprus
Denmark
United Kingdom
Switzerland
Greece
France
Finland
Germany
Italy
Ireland
Poland
Hungary
Sweden
Slovenia
Serbia
Armenia
Malta
Spain
Portugal
Turkey

Citizenship by naturalization

Once your temporary residency and permanent residency periods have been completed, you will be allowed to apply for citizenship through the naturalization process. Long-term residency is a precursor to citizenship through naturalization. As described already, this process takes 10 years and requires the applicant to meet various criteria, depending upon the country. For example, you may be required to take a language proficiency and cultural understanding examination.

Citizenship through marriage

Generally, it takes less time to become a citizen through marriage, but you will still need to pass a language proficiency exam and meet various requirements, depending upon the country.

Citizenship by descent
More than 30 countries around the world allow for citizenship by descent. European countries include Italy, Ireland, France, Hungary, Poland, Germany, and the United Kingdom, among others. The specific requirements vary by country. In general, you have to prove that your ancestor was a citizen in that country and that the citizenship was not renounced in a way that precludes ancestors from seeking citizenship. The rules and the process are complex. Hiring a law firm is a good idea. You will likely need assistance obtaining all of the relevant historical documents, completing the application in the native language, and pursuing the process through the bureaucracy or courts.

Citizenship by investment
Investment is the quickest path to citizenship in Europe. For example, Malta's citizenship by investment program can afford a passport to investors and his/her family within one year. Investors must make a large donation to the country's development fund, which is not returned to the investor. In addition, the applicant must either buy or rent a property for 5 years

Pompeii ruins

and live in it. Lastly, a 6 figure investment in a government approved financial investment (stocks or bonds) is required.

Potential advantages of obtaining a dual-citizenship with an EU country

- Visa-free travel for any length of time across the 28 member states of the EU
- Full working and residential rights in any EU member country
- Subsidized higher education and scholarships
- Ability to set up and grow a business with the benefit of the single economic EU zone without the restrictions faced by non-EU businesses
- Right to consular protection by EU member states when traveling anywhere in the world
- Access to national healthcare benefits
- Right to vote and hold elected office in the country in which one resides as well as in the EU parliament
- Connection to one's heritage and family history
- Privacy is greater in the EU than in other parts of the world
- Fast tracking through customs in the EU citizen queue
- Property ownership in any EU country without a permit

Potential disadvantages of a dual citizenship with an EU country

- The US has a tax treaty with some countries prohibiting double taxation, but check the specific country to which you are connecting
- You become bound by the laws of two countries – the US and your EU country
- The application process for dual citizenship can be long and tedious
- Dual citizens may enlist in the army, but are not permitted to enlist within any military occupational specialty that requires security clearance from the Department of Defense. With regard to the FBI, dual citizens must renounce the foreign citizenship in order to be a special agent.

Swiss guards at the Vatican

Must know information
- US passport should have at least 3 and possibly 6-months validity from planned exit date, depending upon the exit country requirements
- Complete the ETIAS for travel post-January 1, 2022
- Adhere to stay limits within each

259

European country and across the Schengen
- Consider extended stay (e.g., beyond the 90/180 rule) in relevant countries through bilateral agreements
- Apply for a visa while still in the US and apply for residency after entering country
- Consult country government websites for information for longer stay visas, residency, and citizenship

Living or traveling abroad for a period of time may be your life-long dream. Knowing some important parameters regarding time away and length of stay can provide peace of mind during your travels. For further in-depth information, consult the US Department of State's website Travel.State.Gov.

Important Financial Considerations for Longer Stays in Europe

If you're traveling as a tourist, you should have no problems managing finances through the usual means that you use while in the US. However, if you decide to stay for a longer period of time with a residence permit, then you will need to explore the ramifications for investing and paying taxes.

- Choosing a bank for residency in Europe
- Transferring money between the US and Europe
- What to do about US investments while residing in Europe
- Income taxes while residing in Europe

Choosing a bank for residency in Europe

Choose a bank in the US that has a robust online banking option. You'll want to be able to see the transactions in your checking account to regularly balance your checkbook; withdraw money easily from ATMs without fees; send and receive money with a money transfer app, such as Zelle; and communicate with the bank when you have problems or questions.

If you plan on staying in Europe for a very long time, you may consider a foreign bank. However, foreign banks may not be willing to accept you as a client because of a banking law that requires them to report the details f all American account holders to the IRS. This reporting places an extra burden on the bank. One solution is to open an account in the US at a bank with international offices.

t's also wise to maintain a US mailing address for banking, investment, and tax purposes. Using your US address as your residence should eliminate any extra reporting requirements while you're traveling/living in Europe, unless you open a foreign bank account. An expat suggests leaving your financial accounts stateside, but opening a local bank account to pay bills. He has found that Europeans use debit cards much more frequently than credit cards, so it is helpful to have a local account with a debit card.

t is possible to have your Social Security benefits deposited directly into a foreign bank account, but it might be easier to keep all of your transfers and deposits as is in your US financial accounts, and then just transfer money to your local account in Europe as needed. Consider also that your US dollars may be worth more or less than the local currency over time. For example, the US dollar has lost more than 10% of its value against the euro since the coronavirus pandemic took hold. Remember to leave room in your budget for fluctuations in currency exchange rates.

For more details about banking as an expat, consider reading reports from expat bloggers who have moved to Europe from the US. NancyGoesToItaly is a wonderful, informative blog site for US citizens living in Italy. She says that, as an Italian resident, it's wise to change your Italian bank account status to resident, as there are high fees associated with 'stranieri' accounts. The same is likely true for other European countries. She recommends that you keep a US bank account to use for all international transactions. Also, she says to be aware of the United States FBAR and FATCA rules for expats. You must declare any bank balance that exceeds $10,000 during the year. The report is due in April.

- The FBAR (Report of Foreign Bank and Financial Accounts) is a separate form that the Internal Revenue Service requires expats and those with certain foreign bank accounts to file at the same time as, but not with, their regular tax returns.
- "FATCA" is an acronym for the 2010 Foreign Account Tax Compliance

Act. This law requires foreign banks to report their American account holders' details to the IRS. Foreign banks often choose not to take on American clients because of this additional reporting burden.

After purchasing their home and car, Nancy and her husband have made an effort to keep less than 10,000 in the Italian bank account to avoid having to file a report.

Transferring money from your US bank to Europe

You may need to transfer money while you're residing in Europe. Be careful when using your bank or a foreign bank for transfers. They may say that they don't charge any fees, but then instead use a very poor exchange rate. They make money with this internal conversion and you lose money... as much as 7%. Wiring directly from a brick-and-mortar U.S. bank can be costly. Many banks charge an international wire fee as well as giving you a lousy exchange rate.

The better method is to link your U.S. bank account to a third-party app that offers a competitive exchange rate. Consider using relatively new companies such as Transferwise, OFX, and Xoom that allow money to be converted and sent to foreign accounts (and to US accounts) at a relatively low cost by acting as intermediary.

When we needed to make a payment to our citizenship assistance lawyers in Italy, we opted to charge their fees to our American Express card. There was a surcharge of approximately 3%, but we were unfamiliar with other options at the time, and we trusted using American Express for the process. In the future, however, we plan to use Transferwise.

What to do about US investments while residing in Europe
We consulted our financial advisor when we were considering selling our house in Florida and making Italy our permanent home. He said that we would

Stromboli, Italy

need to identify an Attorney-in-Fact (AIF) in the US who could approve all trades, etc. That situation doesn't work well for us, because we are very active in day-to-day trading in one of our brokerage accounts. It would not be feasible to have an intermediary approving those trades. After a lot of careful thought, we decided to maintain our residence in the US.

When Nancy (the NancyGoesToItaly blogger) moved to Italy, she changed the address for their investments to the Italian address. She says, "DO NOT DO THIS. If you do, you will no longer be able to invest in Mutual funds or bond funds. Nor will an advisor be able to help with anything related to investing."

Consult your financial advisor and/or brokerage house to learn the policies for your specific investment firm. But, remember, the law is the same for all US investments, so the policies should be the same across the board, unless the firm has branches in Europe. Nancy says that, in hindsight, she would have changed the addresses to her mail dropbox service located in the United States. After a lot of research, she learned that Schwab has a British presence and will service investment accounts for expats. However, this recently changed. Americans living abroad cannot invest in Mutual funds, ETFs, or stocks at any brokerage at the present time.

In summary, think carefully before deciding to move your permanent residence outside of the United States. In addition to US laws, the EU has also recently passed regulations that affect US expat investors.

Learn more at this informative site https://www.iamadvisors.com/how-do-the-new-eu-priips-rules-affect-us-expat-investors/

Following is an acronym-riddled summary of the EU regulation and how it affects US investors. Even if you don't know the acronyms, you get the gist of what is being said.

Due to the PRIIPs regulation many US investment products are now not legally available to residents of EU countries. They don't have an EU-approved KID, and they cannot legally be sold to EU residents. Many US ETFs for example can't comply with EU PRIIPs legislation because parts of the new rules are contradictory to some US financial regulations. A number of US brokerage firms do not, as yet, seem aware of PRIIPs regulations. However, as awareness spreads it will become increasingly difficult for EU based investors to buy US ETFs or other US funds.

What is the alternative for US expats in the EU? They can try investing in European investment products, but there are complex and potentially expensive US tax ramifications. Also, US expats with over $10,000 in non-US financial accounts, including bank and investment accounts, have to file an FBAR (Foreign Bank Account Report) to FinCEN, and may have to file form 8938 with the IRS depending on the value of foreign financial assets they hold. Beware, foreign investments often trigger onerous US reporting requirements. Failing to comply with the requirements may result in very high fines.

Bottom line, recent EU PRIIPS legislation has resulted in limited access to US funds under EU legislation for many US expat investors living in Europe. The alternative of investing in European funds triggers onerous US reporting requirements that require expensive compliance assistance to avoid fines. It's really important to consult a financial planner who can assist with investing if you are a US expat living in Europe and have investments. The situation will be somewhat different if you have dual citizenship, but, again, it's best to consult the experts in these matters.

Income taxes while residing in Europe

Consult an expert. Hire a tax accountant with expertise in international tax law. You'll still owe US taxes when you live abroad if you are still a US citizen. The US is the only country that taxes citizens no matter where they are living. You must file a U.S. tax return each year, even if it's to report income that you're not required to pay tax on. You must also report balances of foreign bank

Corfu, Greece

accounts if they reached $10,000 at any point during the year, even if for one day.

If you're not working while abroad, paying income tax on employment earnings won't be a concern for you. But you'll still have to pay tax on withdrawals from traditional individual retirement accounts or 401(k)s, taxable pensions and Social Security income over certain income thresholds. Note that U.S. citizens residing in some European countries do not have to pay tax on Social Security benefits because of the specifics of those tax treaties.

Do some research on the relationship between your European residence country and the US with regards to taxes. The US has tax treaties with some countries to prevent double taxation. The tax rules may be different for US citizens who are living off of unearned income (Social Security, pensions, investments, etc.). Living abroad increases the complexity of your tax situation. It's really important to consult a tax professional.

Do some research on the foreign earned income exclusion. You should be eligible. In 2020, the federal tax exclusion applied to the first $107,600 that you earn outside of the US. If you maintain a home in the US, you may still be liable for state income taxes. If you're self-employed, you'll still owe Social Security and Medicare taxes.

Valletta, Malta

CPSIA information can be obtained
at www.ICGtesting.com
Printed in the USA
BVHW091119060122
625602BV00009B/363

 9 781734 484519